Fast & Fabulous
Diabetic
Menus

More than 130 Healthy
& Delicious Recipes for
Special Dietary Needs

BETTY WEDMAN–ST. LOUIS, PH.D., R.D.

CB
CONTEMPORARY BOOKS

Library of Congress Cataloging-in-Publication Data

Wedman–St. Louis, Betty.
    Fast & fabulous diabetic menus : more than 130 healthy & delicious recipes
for special dietary needs / by Betty Wedman–St. Louis.
        p.   cm.
    Includes index.
    ISBN 0-8092-2992-7
        1. Diabetes—Diet therapy—Recipes.   2. High-carbohydrate diet—
Recipes.   3. High-protein diet—Recipes.   4. Vegetarian cookery.
5. Food allergy—Diet therapy—Recipes.   I. Title.   II. Title: Fast and
fabulous diabetic menus.
RC662.W366   1998
641.5′6314—dc21   97-43830
                                                                          CIP

Cover photograph copyright © Chris Cassidy
Cover design by Mary Lockwood

Published by Contemporary Books
A division of NTC/Contemporary Publishing Group, Inc.
4255 West Touhy Avenue, Lincolnwood (Chicago), Illinois 60646-1975 U.S.A.
Copyright © 1998 by Betty Wedman–St. Louis, Ph.D., R.D.
Printed in the United States of America
International Standard Book Number: 0-8092-2992-7
18   17   16   15   14   13   12   11   10   9   8   7   6   5   4   3   2   1

To my colleague, George E. Shambaugh, Jr., M.D.,
whose friendship and guidance have greatly
influenced my nutrition career

CONTENTS

PREFACE

꿏

Yes, it takes time and energy to plan, shop for, and prepare meals. Many people say that planning is the hardest part of mealtimes, so the planning has already been done for you in this book. Whether you follow a high-carbohydrate diet, high-protein diet, "grazer" or snacker regime, or vegetarian diet, or have food allergies, you can find menus and recipes to fit your diabetic diet needs.

The high-carbohydrate diet menus include recipes with sugar in quantities allowed by the American Diabetes Association. Foods such as coffee cakes, cookies, and carrot cakes are no longer "off-limits" when used as part of a diet plan.

The high-protein diet menus minimize the simple carbohydrate choices at a meal without omitting desserts. These menus include a high-quality protein source at each meal to aid in blood-glucose management.

"Grazer" or snacker regimes are included for those who eat on the run because their busy lifestyles seldom provide the time for cooking and sitting down to enjoy a meal. Many of these foods are easy to eat, require few or no eating utensils, and can simply be packed as a "take-along meal."

Vegetarian menus provide variety for the beans and rice lovers. These menu items include both vegan and lacto-ovo vegetarian choices.

This is the first diabetic menu and recipe book to address the needs of those of you with food allergies! It is hard enough to juggle the planning of a diabetic menu, but adding restrictions such as wheat-free, gluten-free, or milk-free can be overwhelming. That has all been done for you with these menus.

Another advantage to *Fast & Fabulous Diabetic Menus* is that it provides menus for different diabetic regimes and allows you to find the one that is right for you. There is no *one* diabetic meal plan. Your menu has to be suited to your individual lifestyle and biochemistry. If your blood-glucose control isn't doing well on the high-carbohydrate–low-fat regime, try the high-protein menus and see if you notice an energy change.

As an added bonus, you will find a Holiday Favorites section that features recipes for Fruitcake, Chocolate Chip Cheesecake, Russian Tea Cakes, and many other traditional delights.

No one has the same diabetic diet needs. You must follow a meal plan that works best for you. *Fast & Fabulous Diabetic Menus* provides you with menus and recipes to do just that!

ACKNOWLEDGMENTS

Many thanks to the hundreds of people with diabetes who have provided the inspiration for these menus and recipes. Unfortunately, they seldom get to taste the recipes they have inspired or contributed to the book.

A special thanks to Susan Busekrus for all her dedication in typing the manuscript. She shared with me how hunger pains and taste buds can be stimulated just by typing the recipes onto a disk.

Howard Bridges and several other friends served as my official tasters and food critics, sampling recipes that didn't always pass inspection on the first attempt. They never complained about calories, fat grams, or overbaked goodies. Through their recommendations, I am able to bring you more than 130 delicious recipes for your diabetic menu enjoyment.

Above all, I am grateful to NTC/Contemporary Publishing and Susan Schwartz, Senior Editor, for the opportunity to provide this comprehensive menu guide for people with diabetes.

INTRODUCTION

❧

We don't eat just to get proteins, carbohydrates, and fats from our food. We eat because we like the taste of certain foods or enjoy the sociability of sharing an eating event. Foods also provide emotional satisfaction.

Let's be realistic about the diabetic diet. Each menu in this book is planned using the basic concept of the six food groups outlined in the Appendix section. These food groups or substitution lists have similar carbohydrate content and nutrient values, but food combinations and menus do not fit perfectly into these six food groups. Food substitutions are made, keeping in mind the calories and carbohydrate content so there will be minimum effect on blood-glucose (blood-sugar) management.

Casserole, stew, salad, and dessert recipes don't usually fit into *exact* exchange patterns for meals. The goal in menu writing featured in *Fast & Fabulous Diabetic Menus* was to keep calories consistent while providing tasty, attractive, and nutritious foods.

Fast & Fabulous Diabetic Menus includes many special-indulgence recipes that have been modified to fit within the diabetic diet—German Chocolate Cake, Snickerdoodles, Chocolate Zucchini Cake, etc. One serving of these indulgences may raise your blood sugar a few points, but you don't need to feel guilty. Planning indulgences can satisfy an emotional need without destroying diabetes control. Instead of having an "all-or-nothing" attitude about enjoying some of your favorite foods, plan to include them in your daily menu so that you avoid feeling as if you have failed or have lost control.

After all, just because you have diabetes doesn't mean you can never eat a cookie again. You'll even find some cookie recipes nutritious enough to be a breakfast food (Tofu-Spice Cookies). Dispense with traditional breakfast foods and try the Baked Date Pudding or Apple Tart with Cheddar Topping once in a while. Food is fun, food is love, and food is to be enjoyed.

My previous cookbook, *Quick & Easy Diabetic Menus*, provided more than 130 delicious recipes for breakfast, lunch, dinner, and snacks. *Fast & Fabulous Diabetic Menus* provides a new approach to diabetic meal planning based on your individual nutritional needs. Some of you prefer a high-carbohydrate diet, others want a vegetarian regime, and an increasing number of you are recognizing that food allergies can complicate your menu planning.

No one menu and recipe book can provide all the answers in diabetic meal planning, but this one is designed to make your eating as exciting and enjoyable as possible. Sugar is not forbidden in a recipe, but keeping fat content under control is important. These recipes are modified to provide tasty foods with a minimum of sugar and fat.

You can show up at your next potluck dinner with a Chocolate Zucchini Cake and announce to all your friends that this is allowed on your diabetic diet. Who said low-sugar and low-fat foods had to taste like cardboard! These recipes will test your self-discipline so keep those portions under control.

The Holiday Favorites section will test your culinary skills and make all your friends marvel at how you can produce low-fat, low-sugar treats everyone can enjoy.

Bon appétit!

MENUS

HIGH-CARBOHYDRATE MENUS

Day 1

Breakfast   Yogurt Streusel Coffee Cake*
Grapefruit half
Beverage of choice

Lunch   California Pizza*
Low-Fat Carrot Cake*
Beverage of choice

Dinner   Parmesan Scallop Delight*
Broccoli Mashed Potatoes*
Arugula-Tomato Salad*
Pineapple Upside-Down Cake*
Beverage of choice

*Recipe included.

Day 2

Breakfast   Breakfast Bar*
Melon wedge
Beverage of choice

Lunch   Fresh Tuna Pasta Salad*
Lentil-Tomato Salad*
Frozen Fruit Delight*
Beverage of choice

Dinner   Seafood Trio*
Sesame-Rice Salad*
Hot Cabbage Slaw*
Banana S'more*
Beverage of choice

*Recipe included.

Day 3

Breakfast	Oatmeal Pancakes*
	Fruit Sauce for Pancakes*
	Beverage of choice
Lunch	Broccoli Quiche*
	California Waldorf Salad*
	Chocolate–Peanut Butter Treat*
	Beverage of choice
Dinner	Beer-Baked Chicken*
	Roast Potato Salad*
	Red Cabbage Slaw*
	White Chocolate Nut Crisp*
	Beverage of choice

*Recipe included.

Day 4

Breakfast   Bran Muffin Classic*
Strawberries
Beverage of choice

Lunch   Gazpacho*
Barbecued chicken
Sesame-Rice Salad*
Fruit Kabob with Chocolate Dip*
Beverage of choice

Dinner   Turkey Salisbury Steak à la Ritz*
Cinnamon Noodle Casserole*
Hot Zucchini and Tomato Salad*
Pumpkin Cream Roll*
Beverage of choice

*Recipe included.

Day 5

Breakfast Crunchy Rice Granola*
Milk or milk substitute
Fresh fruit in season
Beverage of choice

Lunch Tuna salad sandwich
Paradise Salad*
Banana Bread*
Beverage of choice

Dinner Chicken with Gingersnap Sauce*
Potatoes with Roasted Garlic*
Mixed vegetables
Beet Salad with Orange Dressing*
Chocolate Tea Cookie*
Beverage of choice

*Recipe included.

Day 6

Breakfast	Strawberry Smoothie*
	Corn Muffin*
	Beverage of choice
Lunch	Buffalo Stew with Vegetables*
	Mixed vegetable greens
	Raspberry Vinaigrette Dressing*
	Apple Crisp*
	Beverage of choice
Dinner	Chicken Maryland*
	Savory Rice Dressing*
	Broccoli with Sautéed Garlic*
	Hermit cookie*
	Beverage of choice

*Recipe included.

Day 7

Breakfast Teff Banana Muffin*
Vanilla yogurt
Beverage of choice

Lunch Mexican Tortilla Pie*
Mixed salad greens
Raspberry Vinaigrette Dressing*
Beverage of choice

Dinner Hearty Pork Chop and Beans*
Noodles and Peas Supreme*
Spinach
California Waldorf Salad*
Chocolate Zucchini Cake*
Beverage of choice

*Recipe included.

HIGH-PROTEIN
MENUS

Day 1

Breakfast   Venison Sausage*
            Apple-Cinnamon Muffin*
            Orange juice
            Beverage of choice

Lunch   Quinoa Salad*
        Broccoli with Sautéed Garlic*
        Cheese and crackers
        Beverage of choice

Dinner   Broiled Coconut Shrimp*
         Mushroom-Barley Casserole*
         Strawberry-Spinach Salad*
         Baked Rice Pudding*
         Beverage of choice

*Recipe included.

Day 2

Breakfast   Amaranth Granola* with yogurt
Melon wedge
Beverage of choice

Lunch   Lean Minestrone*
Turkey Grape Salad*
Fruit and Rice Delight*
Beverage of choice

Dinner   Beer-Baked Chicken*
Savory Rice Dressing*
Hot Cabbage Slaw*
Fruit Kabob with Chocolate Dip*
Beverage of choice

*Recipe included.

Day 3

Breakfast Spicy Turkey Sausage*
Bran Muffin Classic*
Grapefruit half
Beverage of choice

Lunch Basil and Mozzarella Salad*
Beet Salad with Orange Dressing*
Rice Pulau*
Beverage of choice

Dinner Herbed Pork Kabob
Potatoes with Roasted Garlic*
Broccoli Mélange*
Arugula Tomato Salad*
Frozen Fruit Delight*
Beverage of choice

*Recipe included.

Day 4

Breakfast   Apple Tart with Cheddar Topping*
Beverage of choice

Lunch   Ensalada Arteca*
Blonde Brownie*
Beverage of choice

Dinner   Classic Cioppino*
French bread
Mixed salad greens
Raspberry Vinaigrette Dressing*
Chocolate Tea Cookie*
Beverage of choice

*Recipe included.

Day 5

Breakfast	Strawberry Smoothie*
	Corn Muffin*
	Beverage of choice
Lunch	Ostrich Chili*
	Oyster crackers
	Mixed salad greens
	Raspberry Vinaigrette Dressing*
	Banana Spice Cake*
	Beverage of choice
Dinner	Pistachio-Crusted Chicken Breast*
	Broccoli Mashed Potatoes*
	Hot Zucchini and Tomato Salad*
	Monkey Bar*
	Beverage of choice

*Recipe included.

Day 6

Breakfast   Yogurt Streusel Coffee Cake*
Scrambled egg
Orange juice
Beverage of choice

Lunch   Lebanese Meatballs*
Couscous Salad*
Mixed salad greens with dressing of
choice
Fruit Cocktail Cake*
Beverage of choice

Dinner   Venison Cutlet with Fruit Salsa*
Broccoli Mashed Potatoes*
Hot Zucchini and Tomato Salad*
Tofu-Spice Cookie*
Beverage of choice

*Recipe included.

Day 7

Breakfast   Breakfast Bar*
           Grilled ham slice
           Grapefruit half
           Beverage of choice

Lunch   Fresh Tuna Pasta Salad*
           Arugula-Tomato Salad*
           Blueberry-Tofu Pie*
           Beverage of choice

Dinner   Baked Grouper Florentine*
           Polenta*
           Steamed carrots
           Paradise Salad*
           Pumpkin Cream Roll*
           Beverage of choice

*Recipe included.

"GRAZER" OR SNACKER MENUS

Day 1

Breakfast	Breakfast Bar* Beverage of choice
Lunch	Strawberry Smoothie* Corn Muffin*
Snack	Cheese and Crackers White Chocolate Nut Crisp* Beverage of choice
Dinner	Egg Noodles with Yogurt-Vegetable Sauce* Paradise Salad* Peanut Butter Cookie* Beverage of choice

*Recipe included.

Day 2

Breakfast   Tofu-Spice Cookie*
            Apple
            Beverage of choice

Lunch   Basil and Mozzarella Salad*
        Mediterranean Rice Salad*
        Beverage of choice

Snack   Oatmeal Cookie*
        Venison Chili*
        Beverage of choice

Dinner   Broiled Coconut Shrimp*
         Hot Cabbage Slaw*
         French bread
         Beverage of choice

*Recipe included.

Day 3

Breakfast   Baked Date Pudding*
             Vanilla yogurt
             Beverage of choice

Lunch   Reuben Casserole*
         California Waldorf Salad*
         Rye bread
         Beverage of choice

Snack   Chocolate Chip Bar Cookie*
         Strawberry Smoothie*
         Beverage of choice

Dinner   California Pizza*
          Beverage of choice

*Recipe included.

Day 4

Breakfast   Monkey Bar*
            Beverage of choice

Lunch   Mexican Tortilla Pie*
         Fresh fruit cup
         Beverage of choice

Snack   Venison-Vegetable Meatloaf*
         Crackers
         Lemon Bar*

Dinner   Turkey–Grilled Cheese Sandwich*
          Hot Zucchini and Tomato Salad*
          Snickerdoodle*
          Beverage of choice

*Recipe included.

VEGETARIAN MENUS

Day 1

Breakfast   Tofu Breakfast Pocket*
Beverage of choice

Lunch   Apple Tart with Cheddar Topping*
Mixed salad greens
Raspberry Vinaigrette Dressing*
Beverage of choice

Dinner   Rice and Lentil Patties in Curried
Tomato Sauce*
Broccoli Mashed Potatoes*
Frozen Fruit Delight*
Beverage of choice

*Recipe included.

Day 2

Breakfast   Strawberry Smoothie*
Bran Muffin Classic*
Beverage of choice

Lunch   Bean-Veggie Burger*
California Waldorf Salad*
Beverage of choice

Dinner   Lean Minestrone*
Noodles Romanoff with Tofu*
French bread
German Chocolate Cake*
Beverage of choice

*Recipe included.

Day 3

Breakfast   Breakfast Bar*
             Melon wedge or fresh fruit in season
             Beverage of choice

Lunch   Vegetarian Shepherd's Pie*
         Paradise Salad*
         Brownie*
         Beverage of choice

Dinner   Focaccia*
          Pumpkin Cream Roll*
          Beverage of choice

*Recipe included.

Day 4

Breakfast   Orange Quinoa Muffin*
Yogurt
Beverage of choice

Lunch   Oriental-Style Tofu Sandwich*
Mediterranean Rice Salad*
Beverage of choice

Dinner   Vegetable Bean Soup*
Pasta with Spicy Split Pea Sauce*
Beet Salad with Orange Dressing*
Fruit Kabob with Chocolate Dip*
Beverage of choice

*Recipe included.

FOOD-ALLERGY MENUS: WHEAT-FREE MENUS

Day 1

Breakfast   Oatmeal
Milk
Grapes
Beverage of choice

Lunch   Tuna salad
Rice-Flour Muffin*
Fresh fruit in season
Beverage of choice

Dinner   Baked Grouper Florentine*
Savory Rice Dressing*
Hot Cabbage Slaw*
Oatmeal Cookie*
Beverage of choice

*Recipe included.

Day 2

Breakfast   Amaranth Granola*
Milk or milk substitute
Apple
Beverage of choice

Lunch   Ground beef patty
Broccoli Mashed Potatoes*
Carrot salad
Beverage of choice

Dinner   Beef flank steak
Roast Potato Salad*
Spinach
Arugula-Tomato Salad*
Amaranth Apple Crisp*
Beverage of choice

*Recipe included.

Day 3

Breakfast   Teff Banana Muffin*
Papaya
Beverage of choice

Lunch   Chicken Barley Vegetable Soup*
Cheese and rice crackers
Grapes
Beverage of choice

Dinner   Baked Cornish hen
Cornbread Stuffing*
Peas
Paradise Salad*
Teff Chocolate Chip Cookie*
Beverage of choice

*Recipe included.

Day 4

Breakfast   Orange Quinoa Muffin*
Grapefruit half
Beverage of choice

Lunch   Black Bean Tortilla Casserole*
Strawberry Smoothie*

Dinner   Lamb chop
Baked sweet potato
Broccoli with Sautéed Garlic*
Rice Flour–Applesauce Cake*
Beverage of choice

*Recipe included.

GLUTEN-FREE MENUS

Day 1

Breakfast   Grits
            Scrambled egg
            Cornbread*
            Orange juice
            Beverage of choice

    Lunch   Ensalada Arteca*
            Beverage of choice

   Dinner   Rib-eye steak
            Savory Rice Dressing*
            Spinach
            Beet Salad with Orange Dressing*
            Rice Flour–Chocolate Chip Cookie*
            Beverage of choice

*Recipe included.

Day 2

Breakfast   Strawberry Smoothie*
Rice-Flour Muffin*
Beverage of choice

Lunch   Tuna salad
Mediterranean Rice Salad*
Carrot sticks
Beverage of choice

Dinner   Broiled salmon
Potatoes with Roasted Garlic*
Mixed vegetables
Hot Cabbage Slaw*
Baked Rice Pudding*
Beverage of choice

*Recipe included.

Day 3

Breakfast   Venison Sausage*
Corn Muffin*
Papaya cubes
Beverage of choice

Lunch   Classic Cioppino*
Rice
Paradise Salad*
Beverage of choice

Dinner   Hearty Pork Chop and Beans*
Fresh spinach salad
Raspberry Vinaigrette Dressing*
Rice Flour–Applesauce Cake*
Beverage of choice

*Recipe included.

Day 4

Breakfast   Spicy Turkey Sausage*
            Crunchy Rice Granola*
            Milk or milk substitute
            Beverage of choice

Lunch   Chef's salad
            Raspberry Vinaigrette Dressing*
            Rice crackers
            Frozen Fruit Delight*
            Beverage of choice

Dinner   Baked chicken
            Savory Rice Dressing*
            Broccoli with Sautéed Garlic*
            Arugula-Tomato Salad*
            Rice-Flour Brownie*
            Beverage of choice

*Recipe included.

MILK-FREE/LACTOSE-FREE MENUS

Day 1

Breakfast   Oatmeal
Bran Muffin Classic*
Grapefruit half
Beverage of choice

Lunch   Sliced turkey sandwich
Roast Potato Salad*
Grapes
Beverage of choice

Dinner   Chicken Maryland*
Baked potato
Asparagus
Beet Salad with Orange Dressing*
Oatmeal Cookie*
Beverage of choice

*Recipe included.

Day 2

Breakfast   Crunchy Rice Granola*
  Rice beverage
  Banana slices
  Beverage of choice

Lunch   Fresh Tuna Pasta Salad*
  French bread
  Fresh fruit in season
  Beverage of choice

Dinner   Classic Cioppino*
  Rice
  Hot Zucchini and Tomato Salad*
  Monkey Bar*
  Beverage of choice

*Recipe included.

Day 3

Breakfast   Spelt Biscuit*
            Nut butter
            Orange juice
            Beverage of choice

Lunch   Buffalo Stew with Vegetables*
            California Waldorf Salad*
            Beverage of choice

Dinner   Lebanese Meatballs*
            Sesame-Rice Salad*
            Rice Flour–Chocolate Chip Cookie*
            Beverage of choice

*Recipe included.

Day 4

Breakfast	Scrambled egg
	Orange Quinoa Muffin*
	Strawberries
	Beverage of choice
Lunch	Ostrich Chili*
	Oyster crackers
	Fresh fruit cup
	Beverage of choice
Dinner	Hearty Pork Chop and Beans*
	Savory Rice Dressing*
	Broccoli with Sautéed Garlic*
	Arugula-Tomato Salad*
	Snickerdoodle*
	Beverage of choice

*Recipe included.

EGG-FREE MENUS

Day 1

Breakfast   Amaranth Granola*
            Milk or milk substitute
            Half a grapefruit
            Beverage of choice

Lunch   Fresh Tuna Pasta Salad*
        French bread
        Fruit Kabob with Chocolate Dip*
        Beverage of choice

Dinner   Seafood Trio*
         Sesame-Rice Salad*
         Asparagus
         Beet Salad with Orange Dressing*
         Teff Chocolate Chip Cookie*
         Beverage of choice

*Recipe included.

Day 2

Breakfast   Spicy Turkey Sausage*
Grits
Strawberries
Beverage of choice

Lunch   California Pizza*
Beverage of choice

Dinner   Broiled lamb chop
Quinoa Salad*
Broccoli with Sautéed Garlic*
Rice Flour–Applesauce Cake*
Beverage of choice

*Recipe included.

Day 3

Breakfast   Oatmeal
Milk
Banana slices
Beverage of choice

Lunch   Couscous Salad*
Basil and Mozzarella Salad*
Melon cubes
Beverage of choice

Dinner   Pistachio-Crusted Chicken Breast*
Cornbread Stuffing*
Green beans
Arugula-Tomato Salad*
Rice-Flour Brownie*
Beverage of choice

*Recipe included.

Day 4

Breakfast   Spelt Biscuit*
            Nut butter
            Fresh fruit in season
            Beverage of choice

Lunch   Chicken Barley Vegetable Soup*
            Sliced turkey sandwich
            Frozen Fruit Delight*
            Beverage of choice

Dinner   Turkey Salisbury Steak à la Ritz*
            Potatoes with Roasted Garlic*
            Spinach
            Beet Salad with Orange Dressing*
            Amaranth Apple Crisp*
            Beverage of choice

*Recipe included.

RECIPES

MAIN DISHES

❧

Mexican Tortilla Pie

1 teaspoon vegetable oil
1 clove garlic, minced
½ cup chopped onion
¼ cup chopped green bell pepper
1 14½-ounce can whole peeled
    tomatoes
1 4-ounce can chopped green chili
    peppers
¼ cup tomato paste
2 teaspoons chili powder
1½ teaspoons dried oregano
½ teaspoon ground cumin
¼ teaspoon ground cayenne pepper
½ pound lean ground beef
8 large corn tortillas
1 cup (4 ounces) shredded low-fat
    mozzarella cheese

Combine oil, garlic, onion, and green pepper in skillet. Sauté 5 minutes or until onion is tender. Add tomatoes, chili peppers, tomato paste, chili powder, oregano, cumin, and cayenne pepper. Heat beef in separate skillet until brown, draining off any fat. Add to tomato mixture.

Preheat the oven to 350°F. Oil 9-inch pie pan and line with 4 of the tortillas. Place half of the meat and tomato mixture over the tortillas. Sprinkle with half of the cheese. Lay remaining 4 tortillas over the mixture. Spread on the remaining meat mixture. Top with remaining cheese. Bake 20–25 minutes or until cheese melts and tortillas are brown on edges. Let stand 10 minutes before cutting into wedges.

Makes 4 servings

One serving =   371 calories
                31 g protein
                38 g carbohydrate
                14 g fat
                391 mg sodium
                469 mg potassium
                96 mg cholesterol

One serving =   2 medium-fat proteins + 2 starches/breads
                + 1 vegetable

Lebanese Meatballs

½ *pound lean ground beef*
¼ *pound ground lamb*
½ *cup chopped onion*
⅓ *cup chopped pine nuts*
¼ *cup chopped fresh parsley*
2 *cloves garlic, crushed*
1 *teaspoon ground thyme*
½ *teaspoon salt*
½ *teaspoon curry powder*
¼ *teaspoon freshly ground black
     pepper*
1 *egg*
2 *tablespoons vegetable oil*

Combine beef, lamb, onion, pine nuts, parsley, garlic, seasonings, and egg in a bowl. Mix until well blended. Shape into 1-inch balls. Heat vegetable oil in large skillet. Add meatballs and cook for 10 minutes or until brown and desired doneness is reached. Serve with rice.

Makes 4 servings

One serving (without rice) = 189 calories
                                    15 g protein
                                    7 g carbohydrate
                                    9 g fat
                                    162 mg sodium
                                    291 mg potassium
                                    69 mg cholesterol

One serving = 2 medium-fat proteins

Reuben Casserole

1 16-ounce can sauerkraut, drained
1 cup (4 ounces) shredded
    Swiss cheese
4 ounces corned beef, chopped fine
¼ cup mayonnaise*
1 tablespoon prepared mustard*

Preheat the oven to 350°F. Combine all ingredients and spread in quiche pan or 8-inch square baking pan. Bake 15–20 minutes or until mixture is heated through and cheese melts. Serve warm as main dish or on rye bread as sandwich filling.

Makes 2 servings

One serving = 331 calories
            22 g protein
            8 g carbohydrate
            18 g fat
            896 mg sodium
            714 mg potassium
            181 mg cholesterol

One serving = 3 high-fat proteins + 1 fat

---

*One-fourth cup Thousand Island dressing can be substituted for the mayonnaise and mustard.

Hearty Pork Chops and Beans

3 lean pork chops, about 1 pound
1 16-ounce can Great Northern beans
3 scallions, chopped
½ cup chopped green or red bell
*   pepper*
½ cup sliced fresh mushrooms
½ cup ketchup
1 teaspoon dried basil leaves
¼ teaspoon celery seeds

Preheat the oven to 350°F. Place pork chops in bottom of an 8-inch square baking pan. Top with beans, scallions, pepper, and mushrooms. Combine ketchup, basil leaves and celery seeds. Pour over bean mixture. Cover with baking parchment or foil. Bake 30–35 minutes or until pork chops are tender. Brown by baking, uncovered, 5 minutes longer.

Makes 3 servings

One serving = 218 calories
            26 g protein
            12 g carbohydrate
            4 g fat
            319 mg sodium
            511 mg potassium
            67 mg cholesterol

One serving = 3 medium-fat proteins

Herbed Pork Kabobs

1 pound pork tenderloin
¼ cup apple juice
1 teaspoon dried marjoram leaves
1 teaspoon ground rosemary
1 clove garlic, minced
Orange wedges

Cut pork into 1-inch cubes. Combine remaining ingredients except oranges in shallow pan and add pork cubes. Marinate at room temperature 15–20 minutes. Thread pork onto 4 skewers, reserving marinade. Broil 4 to 5 inches from heat, turning frequently. Baste with marinade. Serve with orange wedges.

Makes 4 servings

One serving = 177 calories
22 g protein
1 g carbohydrate
6 g fat
121 mg sodium
62 mg potassium
75 mg cholesterol

One serving = 3 lean proteins

Pistachio-Crusted Chicken Breast

*2 half boneless, skinless chicken
     breasts
1 tablespoon margarine or butter
3 tablespoons finely chopped
     pistachio nuts*

Preheat the oven to 350°F. Wash chicken pieces. Brush chicken with margarine. Roll chicken in nuts. Bake about 30 minutes or until brown and tender.

Makes 2 servings

One serving = 267 calories
              27 g protein
              2 g carbohydrate
              7 g fat
              76 mg sodium
              97 mg potassium
              81 mg cholesterol

One serving = 3 lean proteins + 1 fat

Beer-Baked Chicken

1 12-ounce can beer
1 3-pound whole chicken
1 tablespoon low-sugar orange
    marmalade
½ teaspoon dried thyme leaves

Preheat the oven to 350°F. Open can of beer and place in center of 8-inch square baking pan. Wash chicken, discarding giblets. Place whole chicken over can of beer, so that beer can fits into cavity of chicken. Brush marmalade over chicken. Sprinkle with thyme. Bake 45–60 minutes or until fork-tender and no blood is seen when chicken is cut at joints. Discard beer.

Makes 4 servings

One serving = 260 calories
             22 g protein
             2 g carbohydrate
             11 g fat
             89 mg sodium
             158 mg potassium
             99 mg cholesterol

One serving = 3 lean proteins

Chicken Maryland

1 3½-pound chicken
2 tablespoons vegetable oil
1 small onion, chopped fine
½ cup chopped green bell pepper
1 clove garlic, minced
1 teaspoon curry powder
½ teaspoon dried thyme leaves
1 15½-ounce can tomato pieces
2 tablespoons currants
2 tablespoons toasted almonds

Cut chicken into serving pieces. Heat chicken in oil in heavy skillet until brown. Add onion, green pepper, garlic, curry powder, thyme, tomatoes, and currants. Reduce heat to low and simmer 20–30 minutes or until chicken is tender. Sprinkle nuts on top just before serving.

Makes 4 servings

One serving = 216 calories
        19 g protein
        11 g carbohydrate
        9 g fat
        241 mg sodium
        342 mg potassium
        76 mg cholesterol

One serving = 3 lean proteins + 1 vegetable + 1 fat

Chicken with Gingersnap Sauce

1 3-pound chicken
1 tablespoon vegetable oil
½ cup chopped onion
½ cup (about 6) crumbled
    gingersnaps
¼ cup wine vinegar
¼ cup brown sugar, packed
2 cups chicken stock or water
1 bay leaf
¼ cup currants

Preheat the oven to 350°F. Cut chicken into serving pieces. Place in bottom of baking pan. Combine remaining ingredients in saucepan and heat thoroughly over low heat until sugar is melted. Pour over chicken. Place in oven and bake 30–40 minutes or until chicken is tender.

Makes 4 servings

One serving = 293 calories
    20 g protein
    27 g carbohydrate
    7 g fat
    208 mg sodium
    197 mg potassium
    98 mg cholesterol

One serving = 3 lean proteins + 2 fruits

Turkey–Grilled Cheese Sandwich

1 teaspoon Dijon mustard
2 slices whole-grain bread
2 1-ounce slices cheddar cheese
1 1-ounce slice turkey ham
1 egg white
1 tablespoon milk or water

Spread mustard on bread slices. Top each bread slice with cheese. Place ham slice on one and top with the other slice. Preheat skillet. Mix egg white and milk in shallow pan. Dip sandwich in mixture to coat both sides. Cook sandwich in skillet over medium heat 3–4 minutes on each side or until bread is toasted and cheese is melted. Serve immediately.

Makes 1 serving

One serving = 295 calories
             18 g protein
             22 g carbohydrate
             11 g fat
             839 mg sodium
             287 mg potassium
             49 mg cholesterol

One serving = 3 lean proteins + 2 starches/breads

Spicy Turkey Sausage

1 *pound ground turkey*
1 *teaspoon ground sage* or
    2 *teaspoons minced fresh*
    sage leaves
1/4 *teaspoon crushed red pepper*
    flakes
1 *tablespoon finely minced garlic*
1/8 *teaspoon ground cumin*
1/2 *teaspoon fennel seeds*

Combine all the ingredients. Shape into sausage patties. Heat in skillet over medium heat 4–5 minutes on each side or until brown. Serve immediately or refrigerate for later use.

Makes 8 two-ounce patties

One serving of 2 patties = 157 calories
        18 g protein
        2 g carbohydrate
        7 g fat
        72 mg sodium
        86 mg potassium
        66 mg cholesterol

One serving = 3 medium-fat proteins

Turkey Grape Salad

2 cups chopped cooked turkey
½ cup chopped celery
½ teaspoon salt
¼ to ½ teaspoon mild curry powder
1 orange
1 cup seedless grapes
¼ cup salad dressing
1 tablespoon shredded coconut,
   toasted

Combine turkey, celery, salt, and curry powder in mixing bowl. Peel and chop orange. Add orange, grapes, and salad dressing to turkey mixture. Toss gently to mix. Sprinkle on coconut just before serving.

Makes 4 servings

One serving = 217 calories
    22 g protein
    16 g carbohydrate
    10 g fat
    238 mg sodium
    397 mg potassium
    61 mg cholesterol

One serving = 3 low-fat meat + 1 fruit

Turkey Salisbury Steak à la Ritz

1 pound ground turkey
½ cup oatmeal
¼ cup chopped onion
½ teaspoon salt
¼ teaspoon pepper
1 egg
¼ cup low-fat plain yogurt
1 teaspoon prepared horseradish

Combine all ingredients except the yogurt and horseradish in mixing bowl. Beat together well. Shape turkey mixture into 1-inch-thick steak. Broil 4 inches from heat until brown, turn over and broil until done, about 3–5 minutes on each side. Top with mixture of yogurt and horseradish just before serving.

Makes 4 servings

One serving = 179 calories
              23 g protein
              8 g carbohydrate
              6 g fat
              188 mg sodium
              59 mg potassium
              71 mg cholesterol

One serving = 3 medium-fat proteins

Ensalada Arteca

SALAD

>2 cups cubed cooked turkey
>6 cups chopped mixed salad greens
>1 cup drained canned kidney beans
>1 cup (4 ounces) shredded cheddar
>   cheese
>2 tomatoes, chopped
>4 scallions, chopped
>½ cup chopped black olives

DRESSING

>½ cup vegetable oil
>½ cup apple cider vinegar
>½ teaspoon ground cumin
>1 tablespoon prepared chili sauce or
>   ½ teaspoon chili powder
>¼ cup chopped fresh cilantro
>Taco chips

Combine turkey, salad greens, kidney beans, cheese, tomatoes, scallions, and olives in mixing bowl. Prepare dressing by blending oil, vinegar, cumin, chili sauce, and cilantro. Pour dressing over turkey mixture. Toss to blend. Serve with taco chips on top.

Makes 6 servings

One serving = 332 calories
>25 g protein
>23 g carbohydrate
>13 g fat
>476 mg sodium
>561 mg potassium
>89 mg cholesterol

One serving = 3 lean proteins + 1 starch/bread + 1 vegetable
>+ 2 fats

Ostrich Chili

1 pound ostrich steak*
1 tablespoon vegetable oil
1 clove garlic, minced
1 small onion, chopped
½ teaspoon dried oregano leaves
¼ teaspoon ground cumin
½ tablespoon chili powder
½ teaspoon salt
1 15½-ounce can red kidney beans
1 15½-ounce can tomatoes
1 8-ounce can tomato sauce

Cut ostrich steak into bite-size cubes. Heat oil, garlic, and onion in skillet until brown, about 5 minutes. Add remaining ingredients. Simmer over low heat 20–30 minutes or until meat is tender.

Makes 4 servings

One serving = 248 calories
            23 g protein
            19 g carbohydrate
            4 g fat
            303 mg sodium
            391 mg potassium
            71 mg cholesterol

One serving = 3 very lean proteins + 1 starch/bread

*Beef round steak can be substituted for ostrich.

Buffalo Stew with Vegetables

1 pound buffalo chunks, cut into bite-
     size pieces*
1 cup chopped onion
2 garlic cloves, minced
4 carrots, peeled, cut into ½-inch
     pieces
2 stalks celery, cut into ½-inch pieces
2 large potatoes, peeled, cut into
     ½-inch pieces
2 cups water
1 teaspoon salt
½ teaspoon freshly ground black
     pepper

Brown buffalo in nonstick pan. Add onion and garlic. Sauté. Add remaining ingredients. Cover and simmer over medium heat 1–1½ hours or until meat is tender.

Makes 4 servings

One serving = 289 calories
             26 g protein
             23 g carbohydrate
             11 g fat
             203 mg sodium
             289 mg potassium
             118 mg cholesterol

One serving = 3 very lean protein + 1 starch/bread
             + 1 vegetable

*One pound beef round steak can be substituted.

Venison Sausage

1 *pound ground venison*
1/2 *teaspoon salt*
2 *teaspoons ground thyme*
2 *teaspoons ground oregano*
1 *teaspoon ground sage*
1/2 *teaspoon ground ginger*

Combine ingredients thoroughly. Refrigerate overnight for maximum flavor. Form into 8 meat patties. Sauté in covered skillet over low heat until thoroughly done, about 5 to 8 minutes.

Makes 8 2-ounce patties

One serving of 2 patties = 171 calories
20 g protein
2 g carbohydrate
2 g fat
189 mg sodium
97 mg potassium
66 mg cholesterol

One serving = 3 very lean proteins

Venison Cutlets with Fruit Salsa

4 venison cutlets
1 tablespoon vegetable oil
1 small ripe papaya, peeled, seeded,
    and cut into ½-inch pieces
1 ripe nectarine, pitted and chopped
2 tablespoons finely chopped red bell
    pepper
1 small scallion, sliced thin
1 tablespoon walnut or vegetable oil
4 tablespoons chopped fresh cilantro
    or basil

Sauté venison cutlets in 1 tablespoon vegetable oil in skillet over medium heat, 15 to 20 minutes. To make the fruit salsa, combine papaya, nectarine, red pepper, scallion, 1 tablespoon walnut oil, and 2 tablespoons of the cilantro or basil in a bowl. Toss gently to mix. When venison cutlets are cooked to desired doneness, sprinkle with remaining 2 tablespoons cilantro or basil. Serve with fruit salsa.

Makes 4 servings

One serving = 218 calories
            22 g protein
            16 g carbohydrate
            4 g fat
            135 mg sodium
            287 mg potassium
            72 mg cholesterol

One serving = 3 very lean proteins + 1 fruit

Venison Chili

1 pound ground venison
½ cup chopped onion
1 teaspoon salt
*½ teaspoon freshly ground black
    pepper*
1 cup tomato sauce
½ cup water
2 tablespoons chili powder
1 14½-ounce can tomatoes, chopped

Sauté venison and onion in skillet over medium heat until brown, about 5 minutes. Add remaining ingredients. Reduce heat to simmer; cook, covered, 30–40 minutes or until meat is tender.

Makes 4 servings

One serving of 1 cup = 145 calories
                        22 g protein
                        8 g carbohydrate
                        2 g fat
                        107 mg sodium
                        84 mg potassium
                        18 mg cholesterol

One serving = 3 lean proteins + 1 vegetable

Venison-Vegetable Meatloaf

1 pound ground venison
1 cup shredded carrot, zucchini,
     onion, and celery
½ teaspoon salt
½ teaspoon freshly ground black
     pepper
1 teaspoon dried basil leaves
¼ cup bread crumbs
½ cup V8 juice

Preheat the oven to 350°F. Combine all ingredients in mixing bowl. Blend together well. Shape into loaf and place in loaf pan. Bake 50–60 minutes or until loaf has shrunk from sides of pan.

Makes 4 servings

One serving = 161 calories
             22 g protein
             9 g carbohydrate
             2 g fat
             124 mg sodium
             172 mg potassium
             20 mg cholesterol

One serving = 3 lean proteins + 1 vegetable

Seafood Trio

*¼ pound grouper, cut into 2-inch
    strips
¼ pound sea bass, cut into 2-inch
    strips
1 3-ounce package smoked salmon,
    cut into strips
1 teaspoon Ranch dressing
2 scallions, chopped fine
½ red bell pepper, chopped fine*

Preheat the oven to 375°F. Wrap grouper and sea bass pieces
with strips of smoked salmon. Place on baking parchment or foil.
Spoon on dressing. Sprinkle scallions and pepper over fish. Seal
edges of parchment well. Bake 8–10 minutes or until fish is fork-
tender.

Makes 2 servings

One serving = 122 calories
            20 g protein
            2 g carbohydrate
            3 g fat
            97 mg sodium
            192 mg potassium
            46 mg cholesterol

One serving = 3 lean proteins

Broiled Coconut Shrimp

1 pound fresh shrimp
1 tablespoon cream of coconut or
     coconut milk
2 tablespoons shredded coconut

Peel and devein shrimp. Rinse. Butterfly by slitting open top of each shrimp. Place on baking sheet. Baste some of the cream of coconut over shrimp with spoon or pastry brush. Broil 3–5 minutes about 5 inches from heat. Remove and baste with remaining cream of coconut. Sprinkle on coconut. Broil 1 minute longer or until coconut is brown.

Makes 2 servings

One serving = 181 calories
                 26 g protein
                 12 g carbohydrate
                 3 g fat
                 67 mg sodium
                 114 mg potassium
                 137 mg cholesterol

One serving = 3 very lean proteins

Baked Grouper Florentine

*1 pound fresh grouper fillets (thin
    end is best)
1 10-ounce package frozen chopped
    spinach, thawed
¼ cup Parmesan Ranch dressing**
*1 egg white, beaten with fork
2 tablespoons finely ground
    macadamia nuts*

Preheat the oven to 350°F. Wash grouper. Drain spinach and press out excess moisture. Combine spinach and dressing. Spoon mixture onto grouper fillets. Roll up and secure with wooden screws or toothpicks. Dip into beaten egg white and roll in ground nuts. Place on lightly oiled baking dish. Bake 20–25 minutes or until fork-tender.

Makes 4 servings

One serving = 218 calories
            23 g protein
            9 g carbohydrate
            8 g fat
            200 mg sodium
            288 mg potassium
            96 mg cholesterol

One serving = 3 lean proteins + 1 vegetable + 1 fat

*Three and a half tablespoons Ranch dressing and 1½ teaspoons grated Parmesan cheese can be substituted.

Parmesan Scallop Delight

1½ *pounds bay scallops**
1 *tablespoon margarine or butter*
1 *tablespoon white wine or apple*
    juice
1 *clove garlic, minced*
⅓ *cup grated Parmesan cheese*

Sauté scallops in skillet with margarine, white wine, and garlic until opaque. Place scallops in glass baking pan or ovenproof serving platter. Sprinkle with cheese. Broil 4 to 5 inches from heat until cheese melts, about 3 minutes.

Makes 4 servings

One serving = 147 calories
            23 g protein
            5 g carbohydrate
            4 g fat
            212 mg sodium
            74 mg potassium
            98 mg cholesterol

One serving = 3 low-fat proteins

*Shrimp can be substituted.

Classic Cioppino

1 tablespoon olive oil
1 cup chopped onion
2 cloves garlic, minced
1 cup diced green bell peppers
4 cups canned or fresh chopped
    tomatoes
1 tablespoon tomato paste
1/4 cup lemon juice
1/4 cup chopped fresh parsley
1/4 teaspoon dried basil or
    1 tablespoon chopped fresh basil
1/4 teaspoon dried oregano
1/2 teaspoon salt
1/2 teaspoon white pepper
6 ounces cod or grouper fish fillet
    (frozen or fresh)
8 ounces cooked shrimp
6 hard-shell clams (optional)

Heat oil in saucepan. Add all ingredients except fish, shrimp, and clams. Simmer 20 minutes. Add fish, shrimp, and clams. Continue cooking over low heat 10 minutes or until seafood is tender.

Makes 6 servings

One serving = 242 calories
    22 g protein
    12 g carbohydrate
    4 g fat
    610 mg sodium
    849 mg potassium
    78 mg cholesterol

One serving = 3 very lean proteins + 2 vegetables

Fresh Tuna Pasta Salad

¼ pound uncooked pasta shells
¼ cup low-fat Italian salad dressing
1 pound fresh tuna steak
½ cup thinly sliced green bell pepper
½ cup thinly sliced red bell pepper
3 scallions, chopped fine
⅓ cup sliced black olives
Leaf lettuce and arugula
3 tomatoes, cut into wedges

Cook shells according to package directions. Drain. Place in bowl. Pour salad dressing over shells. Stir to blend. Chill. When ready to serve, poach tuna in small amount of water in skillet until fork-tender, about 10 minutes. Break into bite-size pieces. Add to pasta along with peppers, scallions, and olives. Line plates with lettuce and arugula. Spoon tuna salad onto plates. Garnish with tomato wedges.

Makes 6 servings

One serving = 291 calories
           30 g protein
           23 g carbohydrate
           6 g fat
           408 mg sodium
           516 mg potassium
           74 mg cholesterol

One serving = 3 very lean proteins + 1 starch/bread
           + 1 vegetable

California Pizza

1 prepared pizza crust
4 ounces pizza sauce
1 pound frozen cooked shrimp,
     thawed
2 tablespoons minced fresh basil or
     1 teaspoon dried basil leaves
2 cups (½ pound) shredded
     Monterey Jack cheese
4 ounces shitake or brown
     mushrooms, sliced thin
2 scallions, sliced thin

Preheat the oven to 425°F. Place pizza crust on baking sheet. Top with pizza sauce. Slice shrimp in half and lay on top of pizza sauce. Sprinkle on basil. Cover shrimp with cheese. Top with mushroom slices and scallions. Bake 10–12 minutes or until crust is golden brown.

Makes 4 servings

One serving = 316 calories
              24 g protein
              38 g carbohydrate
              11 g fat
              487 mg sodium
              516 mg potassium
              82 mg cholesterol

One serving = 2 high-fat proteins + 2 starches/breads
              + 1 vegetable

Vegetarian Shepherd's Pie

MASHED POTATOES

> 8 potatoes, peeled and cut into small
> cubes
> ½ teaspoon salt
> 1 tablespoon butter or margarine
> Milk or cream (optional)

PIE

> ½ cup butter or margarine
> 1 medium onion, chopped fine
> 1 cup finely chopped celery
> 1 cup finely sliced carrot
> 8 cups dry bread cubes
> 2 teaspoons ground sage
> ½ teaspoon dried marjoram leaves or
>   1 teaspoon fresh marjoram
>   leaves
> ½ teaspoon dried thyme leaves or 1
>   teaspoon fresh thyme leaves
> ½ teaspoon celery seeds
> ½ teaspoon salt
> 2 tablespoons minced fresh parsley
> 1½ cups water

Cook potatoes in water to cover. Add salt. Bring to boil, then simmer until tender. Drain. Add 1 tablespoon butter. Mash. Milk or cream may be added (if tolerated).

Preheat the oven to 375°F. Prepare vegetable casserole by sautéing ½ cup butter, onion, celery, and carrot in skillet until celery is tender, about 5 minutes. Stir in bread cubes, sage, marjoram, thyme, celery seeds, salt, parsley, and water. Pour into oiled casserole dish. Top with mashed potatoes. Bake 30–40 minutes or until mashed potatoes are golden.

Makes 4 servings

One serving = 305 calories
               11 g protein
               37 g carbohydrate
               12 g fat
               210 mg sodium
               390 mg potassium
               0 mg cholesterol (margarine)

One serving = 2 starches/breads + 2 fats + 1 vegetable

Black Bean Tortilla Casserole

2 cups coarsely chopped onion
2 cloves garlic, minced
1 cup chopped green bell pepper
1 cup chopped red bell pepper
¾ cup picante sauce
1½ teaspoons ground cumin
2 15-ounce cans black beans, drained
1 14½-ounce can stewed tomatoes,
 undrained and chopped
12 6-inch corn tortillas
1½ cups (6 ounces) shredded
 Monterey Jack cheese
1 cup shredded iceberg lettuce
½ cup seeded, chopped, unpeeled
 tomato
4 tablespoons sour cream

Place large skillet over medium heat until hot. Add onion and garlic and sauté 4 minutes or until tender. Add green and red bell peppers and sauté 3 minutes or until tender. Add picante sauce, cumin, black beans, and stewed tomatoes. Cook 5 minutes, stirring occasionally. Remove from heat and set aside.

Preheat the oven to 350°F. Coat a 13″ × 9″ × 2″ baking dish with vegetable oil. Spoon 1 cup of the bean mixture into the baking dish. Arrange 6 of the tortillas in a single layer over bean mixture; top with ¾ cup of the cheese. Spoon 2½ cups of the bean mixture over the cheese. Arrange the 6 remaining tortillas over the cheese; top with the remaining bean mixture. Bake, covered, for 30 minutes. Uncover and top with the remaining cheese. Bake, uncovered, another 5 minutes or until cheese melts. Let stand 5 minutes before serving. Top with lettuce and tomato. Cut into 4½-inch squares; top each serving with 1½ tablespoons of the sour cream.

Makes 6 servings

One serving = 403 calories
18 g protein
52 g carbohydrate
8 g fat
370 mg sodium
481 mg potassium
78 mg cholesterol

One serving = 3 starches/breads + 2 medium-fat proteins
+ 1 vegetable

Oriental-Style Tofu Sandwich

3 ounces sliced tofu
1 tablespoon plus ¼ teaspoon
    prepared teriyaki sauce
1 teaspoon mayonnaise
Dash sesame seed oil
½ scallion, minced
⅛ teaspoon dried ginger
1 hard roll
2 water chestnuts, sliced thin
¼ cup fresh bean sprouts
¼ cup shredded carrot

Marinate tofu in 1 tablespoon teriyaki sauce while preparing Oriental dressing. To make Oriental dressing, combine mayonnaise, sesame seed oil, remaining ¼ teaspoon teriyaki sauce, scallion, and ginger in mixing bowl. Stir to blend. Broil or sauté tofu until heated, about 3 minutes. Toast roll. Spread top and bottom of roll with Oriental dressing. Place grilled tofu on bottom half. Top with water chestnuts, bean sprouts, carrots, and roll half. Serve immediately.

Makes 1 serving

One serving = 431 calories
             33 g protein
             43 g carbohydrate
             9 g fat
             987 mg sodium
             361 mg potassium
             10 mg cholesterol

One serving = 3 medium-fat proteins + 2 starches/breads
             + 1 vegetable + 1 fat

Focaccia

1 prepared pizza crust
1 tablespoon olive oil
2 fresh tomatoes, sliced thin
3 scallions, chopped fine
1 teaspoon chopped hot peppers*
1 cup (4 ounces) shredded low-fat
    mozzarella cheese
2 tablespoons grated Parmesan
    cheese

Preheat the oven to 425°F. Place pizza crust on baking sheet. Brush with oil. Lay tomato slices over crust. Sprinkle on scallions and peppers. Top with cheeses. Bake 10–12 minutes or until crust is brown and cheese melts.

Makes 4 servings

One serving = 374 calories
           16 g protein
           41 g carbohydrate
           11 g fat
           510 mg sodium
           893 mg potassium
           27 mg cholesterol

One serving = 2 medium-fat proteins + 2 starches/breads

*One-half teaspoon dried hot red pepper flakes can be substituted.

Rice and Lentil Patties in Curried Tomato Sauce

PATTIES

½ cup white long grain rice
3 cups water
⅓ cup green lentils
½ cup finely chopped onion
1 tablespoon olive oil
1 clove garlic, minced
1 tablespoon finely chopped hot
    green chili peppers
1 teaspoon dried cumin seeds
1 egg white

SAUCE

1 cup sliced onion
1 14½-ounce can whole tomatoes
1 8-ounce can tomato sauce
1-inch piece fresh ginger, peeled and
    minced*
1 clove garlic, minced
½ to 1 teaspoon curry powder
¼ teaspoon ground cumin
Chopped fresh cilantro or parsley

Combine rice and 1½ cups water in saucepan. Cook 18–20 minutes or until rice is tender and all liquid is absorbed. Cool. Cook lentils in remaining 1½ cups water for 30–40 minutes or until tender. Drain off any liquid and cool. Sauté ½ cup onion in oil with 1 clove garlic until onion is tender, about 5 minutes. Combine rice, lentils, onion mixture, chili peppers, cumin seeds, and egg white in mixing bowl. Mix well. Shape into 8 patties.

Prepare sauce by cooking 1 cup sliced onion, tomatoes, tomato sauce, ginger, 1 clove garlic, curry powder, and ground cumin in saucepan. Cook over medium heat about 15 minutes, or until reduced to about half. Place rice and lentil patties in lightly oiled skillet. Heat on low until tomato sauce is ready for serving. Top with cilantro or parsley.

Makes 4 servings

One serving of 2 patties = 242 calories
11 g protein
49 g carbohydrate
3 g fat
217 mg sodium
491 mg potassium
2 mg cholesterol

One serving = 3 starches/breads + 1 vegetable

*One-fourth teaspoon ground ginger can be substituted.

Tofu Breakfast Pockets

4 6-inch pita pockets, cut in half
1 cup fresh spinach leaves
8 ounces soft tofu
½ cup alfalfa sprouts
¼ cup low-fat herb vinaigrette salad
*   dressing*

Line each pita pocket with spinach. Crumble tofu and divide into pita pockets. Add sprouts. Top with salad dressing. Serve cold.

Makes 4 servings

One serving = 209 calories
            11 g protein
            28 g carbohydrate
            6 g fat
            291 mg sodium
            186 mg potassium
            0 mg cholesterol

One serving = 1 medium-fat protein + 2 starches/breads

Noodles Romanoff with Tofu

4 ounces egg noodles
1 teaspoon salt
1 small onion, chopped
2 tablespoons margarine or butter
1 tablespoon all-purpose flour
1 clove garlic, minced
1 cup low-fat milk
8 ounces tofu, crumbled
1 ounce grated Parmesan cheese

Cook noodles according to package directions with ½ teaspoon salt. Drain. In a skillet, sauté onion in margarine until tender, about 5 minutes. Add flour, remaining ½ teaspoon salt, and garlic, stirring constantly over medium heat. Cook 3–5 minutes or until thickened. Gradually add milk, stirring constantly. Cook until thickened. Stir in tofu and cheese. Add noodles. Keep warm over low heat until ready to serve.

Makes 4 servings

One serving = 364 calories
22 g protein
36 g carbohydrate
8 g fat
394 mg sodium
286 mg potassium
54 mg cholesterol (margarine)

One serving = 2 medium-fat proteins + 2 starches/breads
+ 1 fat

Bean-Veggie Burgers

1 16-ounce can pinto beans
1 cup dry whole-wheat bread crumbs
2 tablespoons barbecue sauce
¼ teaspoon salt
¼ cup minced onion
½ cup finely chopped green bell
    pepper
1 tablespoon vegetable oil
4 buns

Mash beans and can liquid with potato masher or in food processor. Combine beans, bread crumbs, barbecue sauce, salt, onion,
and green pepper. Mix well. Shape into four burgers. Heat oil in
skillet and sauté burgers until well browned on both sides, about
5 minutes. Serve on buns.

Makes 4 servings

One serving = 265 calories
            10 g protein
            49 g carbohydrate
            3 g fat
            297 mg sodium
            188 mg potassium
            0 mg cholesterol

One serving = 3 starches/breads

Pasta with Spicy Split Pea Sauce

½ cup green split peas
3 cups water
1 clove garlic, minced
2 scallions, chopped fine
½ teaspoon dried hot red pepper
flakes
1½ tablespoons olive oil
1 28-ounce can plum tomatoes
1 bay leaf
2 cups uncooked macaroni
4 tablespoons grated Parmesan
cheese

Combine split peas and water in saucepan. Bring to boil, then reduce heat to medium and cook about 1 hour or until peas are tender. Drain. Sauté garlic, scallions, red pepper, and oil in skillet until scallions are tender, about 5 minutes. Stir in tomatoes and bay leaf. Continue to cook over medium heat until sauce is reduced and thickened. Add the cooked split peas to the sauce. When ready to eat, cook macaroni in large pot of boiling water according to package directions until tender. Drain pasta and place in large serving bowl. Pour sauce over pasta. Top with cheese.

Makes 4 servings

One serving = 372 calories
15 g protein
59 g carbohydrate
8 g fat
398 mg sodium
684 mg potassium
17 mg cholesterol

One serving = 2 very lean proteins + 2 starches/breads + 1 fat

Vegetarian Lasagna

8 *lasagna noodles*
2 *tablespoons oil*
½ *cup chopped onion*
1 *cup thinly sliced carrot*
2 *cloves garlic, minced*
1 *15-ounce jar pasta sauce*
2 *eggs*
2 *cups low-fat cottage cheese*
¼ *cup grated Parmesan cheese*
1 *10-ounce package frozen chopped*
    spinach, thawed and drained
1 *cup shredded part-skim mozzarella*
    cheese

Preheat the oven to 350°F. Prepare lasagna noodles according to package directions. Heat oil in skillet. Add onion, carrot, and garlic. Sauté until carrot is tender, about 5 minutes. Add pasta sauce and set aside. Beat together eggs, cottage cheese, Parmesan cheese, and spinach. Place layer of noodles on bottom of lightly oiled 9-inch-square baking pan. Spread half of the cheese mixture over noodles. Top with remaining noodles. Spread remaining cheese mixture over noodles. Sprinkle on mozzarella cheese. Bake 25–30 minutes or until bubbly around the edges. Let cool 10 minutes before serving.

Makes 4 servings

One serving = 410 calories
            18 g protein
            19 g carbohydrate
            22 g fat
            581 mg sodium
            796 mg potassium
            71 mg cholesterol

One serving = 3 medium-fat proteins + 1 starch/bread
            + 2 vegetables + 1 fat

Basil and Mozzarella Salad

3 *small tomatoes, diced*
¼ cup chopped fresh basil
2 teaspoons olive oil
1 tablespoon white vinegar
½ cup diced part-skim mozzarella
cheese

Mix tomatoes and basil in large salad bowl. Toss in oil, vinegar, and cheese. Let stand for 10 minutes before serving.

Makes 4½-cup servings

One serving = 92 calories
6 g protein
5 g carbohydrate
7 g fat
129 mg sodium
192 mg potassium
11 mg cholesterol

One serving = 1 medium-fat protein + 1 vegetable

Broccoli Quiche

1 10-ounce package frozen cut
    broccoli
1 9-inch frozen prepared piecrust
1/2 cup chopped green bell pepper
1/4 cup chopped onion
1/2 cup (2 ounces) shredded Colby
    cheese
1 cup skim milk
3 eggs
1/2 teaspoon salt
1/4 teaspoon white pepper

Preheat the oven to 350°F. Cook broccoli according to package directions. Drain. Place broccoli in bottom of piecrust. Sprinkle on green pepper, onion, and cheese. Combine milk, eggs, salt, and pepper. Beat well. Pour over broccoli mixture. Bake 30–35 minutes or until set in center. Let stand 5 minutes before serving.

Makes 6 servings

One serving = 297 calories
        14 g protein
        26 g carbohydrate
        13 g fat
        306 mg sodium
        571 mg potassium
        184 mg cholesterol

One serving = 1 starch/bread + 1 high-fat protein
        + 1 vegetable + 2 fats

Oatmeal Pancakes

½ *cup skim milk*
½ *cup low-fat plain yogurt*
½ *cup rolled oats*
⅓ *cup wheat bran*
¼ *cup whole-wheat flour*
1 *egg*
2 *teaspoons sugar*
1 *teaspoon baking powder*
1 *tablespoon vegetable oil*
Fruit sauce or Diet syrup

Combine milk, yogurt, oats, and bran in mixing bowl. Let stand 5 minutes. Add the remaining ingredients and mix until all the flour is combined. Pour ¼ cup of the batter onto lightly oiled griddle or frying pan. Cook about 3 minutes or until bubbles form on edge of pancake. Turn and cook 1½–2 minutes longer. Top with fruit sauce or diet syrup.

Makes 8 pancakes

One serving of 2 pancakes
    (without topping) = 179 calories
                        4 g protein
                        34 g carbohydrate
                        4 g fat
                        141 mg sodium
                        297 mg potassium
                        71 mg cholesterol

One serving = 2 starches/breads

ACCOMPANIMENTS

Chicken Barley Vegetable Soup

2 cups water
¼ cup uncooked pearl barley
1 cup diced cooked chicken
2 cups vegetable juice or tomato juice
1 carrot, chopped
½ cup chopped green bell pepper
1 small onion, chopped
1 clove garlic, minced
1 cup sliced mushrooms
½ cup chopped celery
½ teaspoon salt
½ teaspoon dried thyme leaves
½ teaspoon dried basil leaves
1 bay leaf

Combine all ingredients in large saucepan. Bring to boil; reduce heat and simmer 20–25 minutes or until barley is tender.

Makes 6 servings

One serving = 59 calories
2 g protein
13 g carbohydrate
0 mg fat
495 mg sodium
678 mg potassium
10 mg cholesterol

One serving = 1 starch/bread

Vegetable Bean Soup

1 15½-ounce can red kidney beans
1 15½-ounce can garbanzo beans
2 cups water
2 medium potatoes, peeled and diced
1 cup sliced carrot
½ cup chopped onion
1 clove garlic, minced
1 6-ounce can tomato sauce
2 teaspoons chili powder
1 teaspoon salt
1 teaspoon dried basil leaves

Combine all ingredients in large saucepan. Bring to boil; reduce heat to simmer. Cook 30 minutes or until vegetables are tender.

Makes 6 servings

One serving = 158 calories
8 g protein
36 g carbohydrate
1 g fat
340 mg sodium
682 mg potassium
0 mg cholesterol

One serving = 2 starches/breads

Lean Minestrone

10 *cherry tomatoes, cut in half*
1 *small zucchini, chopped*
1 *small potato, chopped*
1 *onion, chopped*
1 *stalk celery, sliced*
1 *carrot, chopped fine*
1 *clove garlic, minced*
1 *tablespoon finely minced fresh
    parsley*
½ *teaspoon dried thyme leaves* or
    1 *teaspoon minced fresh thyme*
½ *cup cooked or canned Great
    Northern beans*
2 *cups chicken broth*

Combine all ingredients in a saucepan and simmer uncovered for 20 minutes or until vegetables are tender. Ladle into bowls and sprinkle with additional chopped parsley.

Makes 2 servings

One serving = 128 calories
            5 g protein
            22 g carbohydrate
            1 g fat
            49 mg sodium
            273 mg potassium
            0 mg cholesterol

One serving = 1 starch/bread

G a z p a c h o

4 ripe tomatoes, peeled and seeded
1 small cucumber, peeled and seeded
½ cup chopped celery
½ green bell pepper, chopped
¼ cup chopped onion
1 clove garlic, minced
1 teaspoon salt
¼ teaspoon white pepper
2 tablespoons red wine vinegar
½ cup vegetable juice (V8 or tomato
  juice)
Chopped fresh parsley leaves

Combine all ingredients except parsley leaves in blender or food processor. Blend until almost smooth. Chill thoroughly. Serve cold with parsley leaves sprinkled on top.

Makes 4 servings

One serving of 1 cup = 32 calories
                       1 g protein
                       8 g carbohydrate
                       0 mg fat
                       121 mg sodium
                       381 mg potassium
                       0 mg cholesterol

One serving = 1 vegetable

Paradise Salad

DRESSING

> ½ cup coconut milk
> 1 tablespoon mayonnaise
> ¼ cup vanilla yogurt

SALAD

> 2 cups mixed salad greens
> 1 11-ounce can mandarin oranges,
>   drained
> 12 to 15 grapes, cut in half
> Grated toasted coconut (optional)

To make the dressing, combine all ingredients in mixing bowl. Mix thoroughly.

Divide salad greens among four serving plates. Top with mandarin oranges and grapes. Spoon on dressing just before serving. Sprinkle with coconut as garnish.

Makes 4 servings

One salad serving = 74 calories
                    11 g protein
                    24 g carbohydrate
                    2 g fat
                    137 mg sodium
                    394 mg potassium
                    18 mg cholesterol

One serving with dressing = 2 fruits + 1 vegetable

One dressing serving = 48 calories
                1 g protein
                12 g carbohydrate
                1 g fat
                106 mg sodium
                92 mg potassium
                18 mg cholesterol

One serving = 1 fruit

Fruit and Rice Delight

2 cups sliced, cored unpeeled apples
½ cup chopped scallions
1 cup thinly sliced carrot
2 tablespoons vegetable oil
½ cup raisins
2 cups cooked brown rice
½ teaspoon salt
1 tablespoon toasted sesame seeds

Sauté apples, scallions, and carrot in oil in skillet about 10 minutes or until carrot is tender. Stir in raisins, rice, and salt. Cook until rice is heated. Add sesame seeds and toss lightly.

Makes 6 servings

One serving = 162 calories
3 g protein
27 g carbohydrate
6 g fat
217 mg sodium
312 mg potassium
0 mg cholesterol

One serving = 1 starch/bread + 1 fruit + 1 fat

Strawberry Spinach Salad

2½ *cups* (1 *pint*) *sliced fresh*
   strawberries
2 *tablespoons orange juice*
2 *tablespoons red wine vinegar*
2 *tablespoons vegetable oil*
¼ *cup low-fat vanilla yogurt*
10 *ounces fresh spinach leaves*
½ *to* 1 *cup alfalfa sprouts*
Chopped fresh cilantro

Combine ½ cup of the strawberries, the orange juice, vinegar,
oil, and yogurt in blender. Puree. Divide spinach onto four salad
plates. Spoon on dressing. Add the remaining strawberry slices.
Top with alfalfa sprouts. Sprinkle on cilantro.

Makes 4 servings

One serving = 95 calories
               1 g protein
               13 g carbohydrate
               6 g fat
               48 mg sodium
               113 mg potassium
               0 mg cholesterol

One serving = 1 vegetable + 1 fat + ½ fruit

California Waldorf Salad

1 red apple, cored and chopped
1 green apple, cored and chopped
½ cup red grapes
½ cup green grapes
½ cup toasted slivered almonds
¼ cup golden raisins
½ cup vanilla yogurt
¼ cup apple juice
1 teaspoon grated lime zest
1 teaspoon honey
¼ teaspoon ground nutmeg

Toss all ingredients together in salad bowl. Cover and refrigerate until ready to serve.

Makes 4 servings

One serving = 206 calories
5 g protein
33 g carbohydrate
4 g fat
69 mg sodium
291 mg potassium
3 mg cholesterol

One serving = 2 fruits + 1 fat

Mediterranean Rice Salad

1 cup uncooked brown or basmati
    rice
2 cups water
2 tablespoons olive oil
2 cups sliced zucchini (¼-inch slices)
1 teaspoon dried basil
1 teaspoon dried oregano
4 cups red leaf or romaine lettuce
1 cup chopped fresh spinach leaves
1 cup chopped arugula leaves
½ cup sliced black olives
⅓ cup oil and vinegar–type salad
    dressing

Cook rice in water. Add 1 tablespoon of the olive oil to the water. Bring to a boil; simmer, covered, 25–30 minutes or until tender, depending on type of rice used. Combine the remaining 1 tablespoon olive oil and the zucchini in skillet. Add basil and oregano. Sauté until zucchini is slightly brown, about 3 minutes. Break lettuce into bite-size pieces and toss with chopped spinach and arugula leaves. Add rice, zucchini, olives, and salad dressing. Toss well. Serve immediately.

Makes 4 servings

One serving = 231 calories
              4 g protein
              24 g carbohydrate
              12 g fat
              297 mg sodium
              384 mg potassium
              0 mg cholesterol

One serving = 1 starch/bread + 2 vegetables + 2 fats

Couscous Salad

2 cups couscous
2 cups boiling water
¼ cup lemon juice
2 to 4 cloves garlic, minced
2 teaspoons ground cumin
½ teaspoon salt
¼ teaspoon cayenne pepper
3 tablespoons olive oil
¼ cup pine nuts
½ cup shredded carrot
1 cup chopped red bell pepper
½ cup minced fresh parsley
½ cup currants

Place couscous in large mixing bowl. In a separate bowl, mix together the boiling water, lemon juice, garlic, cumin, salt, cayenne pepper, and 2 tablespoons of the olive oil. Pour mixture over couscous, stir and let stand. Sauté pine nuts in the remaining tablespoon of olive oil until golden, about 2 minutes. Add pine nuts to couscous along with remaining ingredients. Let stand 15 minutes. Toss with fork. Chill until ready to serve with favorite entree.

Makes 8 servings

One serving = 171 calories
                4 g protein
                26 g carbohydrate
                8 g fat
                219 mg sodium
                311 mg potassium
                0 mg cholesterol

One serving = 1 starch/bread + 1 vegetable + 1 fat

Lentil-Tomato Salad

2 cups cooked lentils
¼ cup olive oil
¼ cup vinegar
3 scallions, chopped
1 tomato, seeded and diced
1 carrot, peeled and chopped
Salt and pepper
Fresh parsley or cilantro, chopped

Combine lentils, oil, vinegar, scallions, tomato, and carrot in mixing bowl. Toss well. Season to taste with salt and pepper. Sprinkle on parsley just before serving. May be served at room temperature or chilled.

Makes 4 servings

One serving of ½ cup = 159 calories
4 g protein
19 g carbohydrate
11 g fat
47 mg sodium (without salt)
96 mg potassium
0 mg cholesterol

One serving = 1 starch/bread + 2 fats

Rice Pulau

1 large onion, chopped
½ teaspoon ground cinnamon
¼ teaspoon ground cloves
¼ teaspoon ground cardamom
¼ teaspoon ground ginger
½ teaspoon salt
1 tablespoon vegetable oil
1 cup uncooked white rice
2 cups water
½ cup frozen green peas

Sauté onion, spices, and salt in oil in large skillet or saucepan until onion is tender, about 5 minutes. Add rice and water. Cook, covered, 15–20 minutes or until rice is tender. Add peas and cook 5 minutes longer.

Makes 6 servings

One serving = 104 calories
              3 g protein
              18 g carbohydrate
              3 g fat
              184 mg sodium
              197 mg potassium
              0 mg cholesterol

One serving = 1 starch/bread

Sesame Rice Salad

2 cups uncooked brown rice
2 tablespoons sesame seeds, toasted*
2 tablespoons chopped scallion
2 tablespoons tamari

Cook rice according to package directions. When rice is fluffy, combine rice, sesame seeds, scallion, and tamari in mixing bowl. Toss while warm to blend flavors. Serve warm or cold.

Makes 6 servings

One serving = 161 calories
              3 g protein
              27 g carbohydrate
              3 g fat
              217 mg sodium
              196 mg potassium
              9 mg cholesterol

One serving = 2 starches/breads

*Sesame seeds can be toasted in a dry skillet over medium heat or in a toaster oven until they turn brown.

Quinoa Salad

1 cup uncooked quinoa
½ cup chopped red bell pepper
1 scallion, chopped fine
1 tablespoon finely chopped cilantro
1 15½-ounce can black beans,
*   drained*
2 tablespoons olive oil
1 tablespoon balsamic vinegar
2 teaspoons dried oregano leaves
½ teaspoon salt

Cook quinoa according to package directions. Drain and place in mixing bowl. Add red pepper, scallion, cilantro, and black beans. Combine olive oil, vinegar, oregano, and salt in mixing bowl. Beat to blend before pouring over quinoa. Toss ingredients well and refrigerate until ready to serve.

Makes 6 servings

One serving = 203 calories
              2 g protein
              36 g carbohydrate
              7 g fat
              186 mg sodium
              209 mg potassium
              0 mg cholesterol

One serving = 2 starches/breads + 1 fat

Beet Salad with Orange Dressing

*2 pounds fresh beets (about 8 large)** *
Water
¼ cup vegetable oil
¼ cup orange juice
2 tablespoons wine vinegar
Grated zest of 1 orange
*1 package Equal*** sweetener or*
      2 teaspoons sugar
½ cup chopped toasted walnuts

Cook beets in water about 40 minutes or until tender. Rinse under cold water. Peel off skins. Slice beets thin; then cut into julienne strips. Combine oil, orange juice, vinegar, grated zest, and sweetener in small bowl. Beat well. Pour dressing over beets. Toss. Refrigerate 1–2 hours or overnight before serving. Sprinkle on nuts just before serving.

Makes 6 servings

One serving = 94 calories
            1 g protein
            32 g carbohydrate
            12 g fat
            209 mg sodium
            314 mg potassium
            0 mg cholesterol

One serving = 1 vegetable + 2 fats

*One 16-ounce can of whole beets can be substituted.
**Equal is a brand name for low-calorie sweetener aspartame.

Hot Zucchini and Tomato Salad

1 tablespoon butter or margarine
½ small onion, chopped
2 cups thinly sliced zucchini
2 small tomatoes, diced
½ teaspoon dried basil
¼ teaspoon salt, optional

Melt butter in skillet over medium heat. Add onion and sauté 2 minutes. Add zucchini and continue to sauté for 2 more minutes before adding tomatoes and basil. Cook, covered, 2 minutes or until vegetables are tender.

Makes 2 servings

One serving = 58 calories
2 g protein
8 g carbohydrate
4 g fat
16 mg sodium
410 mg potassium
0 mg cholesterol

One serving = 1 vegetable + 1 fat

Arugula-Tomato Salad

3 bunches (about 1 pound) arugula
10 to 12 cherry tomatoes, cut in half
1 carrot, shredded
1 clove garlic
¼ teaspoon salt
1 scallion, minced (white part only)
2 tablespoons balsamic vinegar
3 tablespoons olive oil

Trim arugula and tear leaves in half. Toss arugula, tomatoes, and carrots together. Combine remaining ingredients in blender or food processor. Puree until smooth. Drizzle over salad. (Dressing may be made 1–2 days ahead and chilled in covered container. For best flavor, serve at room temperature and stir well before pouring over salad.)

Makes 6 servings

One serving = 55 calories
      1 g protein
      2 g carbohydrate
      7 g fat
      176 mg sodium
      297 mg potassium
      0 mg cholesterol

One serving = 1 vegetable + 1 fat

Roast Potato Salad

2 pounds (about 6 cups) small red
      potatoes, cut in half
1 tablespoon olive oil
1 tablespoon fresh thyme leaves or
      1½ teaspoons dried thyme
      leaves
1 green bell pepper, cut into thin
      strips
1 small onion, chopped
½ red bell pepper, cut into thin
      strips
2 tablespoons wine vinegar
⅛ teaspoon freshly ground white
      pepper
1 bunch arugula or 2 cups mixed
      salad greens

Preheat the oven to 400°F. Toss potatoes with oil and thyme. Place in baking pan large enough for single layer of potatoes. Bake 15–18 minutes or until fork-tender. Combine green pepper, onion, red pepper, vinegar, and white pepper in bowl. Toss to blend. Add pepper mixture to potatoes in baking pan. Stir to blend potatoes and pepper mixture. Set aside to cool while preparing arugula or salad greens. Serve potato salad on bed of greens.

Makes 6 servings

One serving = 199 calories
                4 g protein
                28 g carbohydrate
                5 g fat
                25 mg sodium
                61 mg potassium
                0 mg cholesterol

One serving = 1 starch/bread + 1 vegetable + 1 fat

Hot Cabbage Slaw

½ pound (1 small head) fresh
cabbage, shredded
½ cup coleslaw dressing
¼ teaspoon prepared mustard
¼ teaspoon dried celery seeds

Place shredded cabbage in mixing bowl. Combine remaining ingredients in saucepan or microwave. Heat thoroughly. Pour over cabbage. Toss well. Serve immediately.

Makes 4 servings

One serving = 58 calories
1 g protein
18 g carbohydrate
8 g fat
311 mg sodium
294 mg potassium
4 mg cholesterol

One serving = 1 vegetable + 1 fat

Red Cabbage Slaw

*4 cups shredded red cabbage (about
    ¾ pound)*
2 apples, cored and chopped fine
¼ cup red wine vinegar
2 tablespoons vegetable oil
1 tablespoon honey
½ teaspoon salt
¼ teaspoon ground nutmeg

Place cabbage and apples in serving bowl. Combine remaining ingredients to make dressing. Pour dressing over cabbage and apple mixture. Toss to blend. Serve immediately.

Makes 6 servings

One serving of ½ cup = 67 calories
    1 g protein
    8 g carbohydrate
    4 g fat
    72 mg sodium
    197 mg potassium
    0 mg cholesterol

One serving = 1 vegetable + 1 fat

Egg Noodles with Yogurt-Vegetable Sauce

8 ounces uncooked egg noodles
1 small onion, chopped
1 clove garlic, minced
½ cup sliced mushrooms
½ cup thinly sliced carrot
½ cup finely chopped green bell
        pepper
1 tablespoon vegetable oil
1 cup low-fat plain yogurt
1 cup diced cooked turkey
Chopped fresh parsley

Cook noodles according to package directions. Drain and pour into serving dish. Sauté onion, garlic, mushrooms, carrot, and green pepper in vegetable oil until tender, about 5 minutes. Stir in yogurt and turkey. Heat thoroughly over low temperature. Pour vegetable sauce over noodles. Sprinkle with parsley. Serve hot.

Makes 4 servings

One serving = 301 calories
            14 g protein
            36 g carbohydrate
            12 g fat
            186 mg sodium
            297 mg potassium
            64 mg cholesterol

One serving = 2 low-fat proteins + 2 starches/breads

Noodles and Peas Supreme

2 ounces uncooked noodles
½ cup frozen peas
2½ cups boiling water
4 tablespoons low-fat Italian dressing
1 tablespoon chopped pimiento

Cook noodles and peas in water for 5 minutes or until noodles and peas are tender. Drain. Add dressing and pimiento. Toss gently to mix. Serve hot or cold.

Makes 2 servings

One serving = 167 calories
4 g protein
28 g carbohydrate
4 g fat
206 mg sodium
311 mg potassium
0 mg cholesterol

One serving = 2 starches/breads + 1 fat

Cinnamon Noodle Casserole

1½ cups cooked noodles
¼ cup raisins
1 egg
2 teaspoons sugar
½ cup apple juice
¼ teaspoon ground cinnamon
⅛ teaspoon ground nutmeg
1 tablespoon chopped pecans

Preheat the oven to 350°F. Place noodles and raisins in lightly oiled 8-inch square baking pan. Combine egg, sugar, apple juice, cinnamon, and nutmeg in mixing bowl. Beat well. Pour over noodles. Sprinkle on nuts. Bake 30–35 minutes or until brown and set in center.

Makes 4 servings

One serving = 132 calories
4 g protein
21 g carbohydrate
3 g fat
72 mg sodium
206 mg potassium
77 mg cholesterol

One serving = 1 starch/bread + ½ fruit

Potatoes with Roasted Garlic

6 medium potatoes
Water
1 teaspoon salt
1 bulb garlic
1 tablespoon margarine or butter
Chopped parsley

Preheat the oven to 350°F. Wash potatoes, removing sprouts and blemishes. Peel and cut into cubes. Cover with water, add salt, and cook over medium heat 15–20 minutes or until tender. Drain well. While potatoes are cooking, roast garlic until soft. Peel and add to drained potatoes with margarine. Mash until smooth. Sprinkle with parsley before serving.

Makes 4 servings

One serving = 87 calories
1 g protein
19 g carbohydrate
3 g fat
126 mg sodium
247 mg potassium
0 mg cholesterol (margarine)

One serving = 1 starch/bread + 1 fat

Broccoli Mashed Potatoes

1½ cups small red potatoes
Water
½ teaspoon salt
1 large stalk broccoli
1 small onion, chopped
1 tablespoon olive oil
2 to 4 tablespoons low-fat plain
         yogurt
½ teaspoon salt

Wash potatoes but do not peel. Cover with water. Add salt and boil in covered saucepan about 15 minutes or until fork-tender. Wash broccoli and cut stem and florets into small chunks. Add to potatoes. Cook until fork-tender. Drain. Sauté onion in oil until soft, about 5 minutes. Combine potatoes, broccoli, onion, yogurt, and salt in food processor and process until smooth. Serve immediately.

Makes 4 servings

One serving = 156 calories
              4 g protein
              29 g carbohydrate
              5 g fat
              189 mg sodium
              341 mg potassium
              4 mg cholesterol

One serving = 1 starch/bread + 1 vegetable + 1 fat

Mushroom-Barley Casserole

1 cup sliced fresh mushrooms
½ cup chopped onion
2 tablespoons vegetable oil
4 cups chicken, turkey, or beef stock
1 cup pearl barley
1 teaspoon salt
Chopped fresh parsley

Sauté mushrooms and onion in vegetable oil in a 2-quart skillet until light brown, about 5 minutes. Add chicken stock (water may be substituted for vegetarian selection), barley, and salt. Cook, covered, over medium heat 30–40 minutes or until barley is tender. Top with parsley just before serving.

Makes 6 servings

One serving of ½ cup = 169 calories
3 g protein
27 g carbohydrate
7 g fat
127 mg sodium
109 mg potassium
10 mg cholesterol (using meat stock)

One serving = 1 starch/bread + 1 vegetable + 1 fat

Broccoli Mélange

1 cup fresh broccoli, cut into 1-inch
        pieces
½ cup sliced fresh mushrooms
1 tablespoon vegetable oil
½ cup thin red bell pepper strips
½ cup sliced yellow summer squash
½ cup sliced zucchini squash
Salt and pepper to taste

Sauté broccoli and mushrooms in vegetable oil until mushrooms are light brown, about 5 minutes. Add remaining ingredients. Cover and simmer 5–10 minutes or until vegetables are tender. Serve immediately.

Makes 4 servings

One serving = 48 calories
          1 g protein
          4 g carbohydrate
          4 g fat
          47 mg sodium (no salt added)
          89 mg potassium
          0 mg cholesterol

One serving = 1 vegetable + 1 fat

Broccoli with Sautéed Garlic

1 pound broccoli
2 cloves garlic, minced
3 tablespoons olive oil
2 tablespoons grated Romano cheese

Cook broccoli until fork-tender. Run cold water over broccoli to stop cooking process. Place broccoli in mixing bowl. Sauté garlic in olive oil until tender and golden brown, about 2 minutes. Sprinkle cheese over broccoli. Pour garlic and olive oil on top of broccoli. Toss gently to coat. Serve at room temperature or chilled.

Makes 4 servings

One serving = 69 calories
          1 g protein
          6 g carbohydrate
          8 g fat
          188 mg sodium
          392 mg potassium
          20 mg cholesterol

One serving = 1 vegetable + 1 fat

Polenta

1 cup cornmeal
1 cup cold water
½ teaspoon salt
3 cups boiling water
¼ cup grated Parmesan cheese
Paprika

Combine cornmeal, cold water, and salt in bowl. Mix well. Stir into boiling water with wire whisk to prevent lumping. Cook over medium heat 15–20 minutes or until thick. Stir occasionally to prevent sticking. Add cheese. Press into lightly oiled loaf pan and keep warm until ready to serve. When ready to serve, remove from pan and cut into slices. Top with paprika just before serving. If making for future use, refrigerate polenta in loaf pan until firm. Remove from pan. Wrap in plastic wrap and store refrigerated until needed. Heat under broiler 4 to 5 inches from heat for 3–4 minutes to serve warm.

Makes 6 servings

One serving = 98 calories
              6 g protein
              19 g carbohydrate
              2 g fat
              117 mg sodium
              67 mg potassium
              29 mg cholesterol

One serving = 1 starch/bread

Cornbread Stuffing

6 *cups cornbread crumbs (or see*
    Corn Muffins or Cornbread
    recipe in Index)
1½ *cups chopped onion*
1½ *cups chopped celery and celery*
    leaves
1 *cup diced mushrooms*
½ *cup vegetable oil*
1 *tablespoon poultry seasoning*
1 *tablespoon salt*
½ *teaspoon pepper*
1 *cup water,* **turkey,** *or chicken broth*

Bake double cornbread or muffin recipe in 8-inch square pan. Let cool. Break into fine crumbs onto baking sheet. Dry out for half an hour in a 200°F oven. Sauté onion and celery in vegetable oil about 5 minutes. Add seasonings and liquid. Pour over crumbs and mix until crumbs are moistened. Stuff turkey and bake immediately or bake separately in 2-quart, greased casserole.

Makes enough stuffing for a 12-pound turkey

One serving of ½ cup = 135 calories
                  2 g protein
                  24 g carbohydrate
                  7 g fat
                  117 mg sodium
                  204 mg potassium
                  0 mg cholesterol

One serving = 1 starch/bread + 1 fat

Savory Rice Dressing

1 cup cooked brown rice
2 teaspoons vegetable oil
½ cup diced celery
¼ cup chopped scallion
2 tablespoons fresh parsley or
       1 tablespoon dried parsley flakes
¼ teaspoon salt
¼ teaspoon sage
1 cup sliced fresh mushrooms
½ cup artichoke hearts
1 cup chicken broth or tomato juice

Sauté rice in vegetable oil until light brown. Add celery, scallion, parsley, salt, sage, mushrooms, and artichoke hearts. Sauté 2 minutes longer. Add chicken broth and mix into moistened rice. Heat, covered, over medium heat 15 minutes or preheat the oven to 325°F and pour the mixture into casserole dish and bake 20 minutes.

Makes 4 servings

One serving = 98 calories
       2 g protein
       18 g carbohydrate
       2 g fat
       114 mg sodium
       143 mg potassium
       0 mg cholesterol

One serving = 1 starch/bread + 1 vegetable

Raspberry Vinaigrette Dressing

1½ *cups fresh raspberries*
1 *tablespoon sugar*
¼ *teaspoon dried whole thyme*
¼ *teaspoon freshly ground black*
    pepper
3 *tablespoons white wine vinegar*
3 *tablespoons water*
2 *teaspoons vegetable oil*
Salad greens

Combine all ingredients in container of an electric blender. Cover and process until mixture is smooth. Strain raspberry mixture to remove seeds. Cover and chill thoroughly. Serve with salad greens.

Makes 1 cup

One serving = 12 calories
            o mg protein
            2 g carbohydrate
            o mg fat
            19 mg sodium
            56 mg potassium
            o mg cholesterol

One serving = Free

Fruit Sauce for Pancakes

¼ cup raisins
¼ cup boiling water
4 ripe bananas
1 orange, peeled and seeded
1 tablespoon lemon juice

Place raisins and boiling water in blender or food processor. Let stand about 5 minutes or until raisins are plump. Add remaining ingredients. Puree until smooth. Serve on pancakes, French toast, or waffles.

Makes 1½ to 2 cups

One serving of ¼ cup = 78 calories
1 g protein
15 g carbohydrate
1 g fat
45 mg sodium
291 mg potassium
0 mg cholesterol

One serving = 1 fruit

BREADS AND DESSERTS

Low-Fat Carrot Cake

2 cups grated carrot
¾ cup sugar
1 8-ounce can juice-packed crushed
        pineapple
½ cup unsweetened applesauce
2 tablespoons vegetable oil
4 egg whites
2 cups all-purpose flour
1 tablespoon baking powder
1½ teaspoons ground cinnamon
½ teaspoon ground nutmeg
½ cup shredded coconut
4 ounces low-fat cream cheese,
        softened
1 cup low-fat whipped topping
¼ cup chopped walnuts

Preheat the oven to 375°F. In a large mixing bowl, combine carrot, sugar, pineapple with juice, applesauce, oil, and egg whites. Stir to blend thoroughly. Add flour, baking powder, cinnamon, nutmeg, and coconut. Mix well. Pour batter into lightly oiled 9″ × 13″ baking pan. Bake 35–40 minutes or until toothpick inserted into center comes out clean. Let cool thoroughly on rack. Beat cream cheese with wire whisk until fluffy. Stir in whipped topping. Spread on top of cake. Sprinkle on nuts.

Makes 16 servings

One serving = 243 calories
     3 g protein
     32 g carbohydrate
     13 g fat
     186 mg sodium
     316 mg potassium
     4 mg cholesterol

One serving = 1 starch/bread + 2 fats + 1 fruit

Rice Flour–Applesauce Cake

2 cups brown rice flour*
2 tablespoons potato starch*
½ cup sugar
1 tablespoon baking powder
1 teaspoon ground cinnamon
½ teaspoon ground nutmeg
½ cup applesauce
½ cup apple juice
⅓ cup vegetable oil

Preheat the oven to 375°F. Combine all ingredients in mixing bowl. Pour batter into lightly oiled 8-inch square baking pan. Bake 15–20 minutes. Let cool. Cut into squares.

Makes 12 servings

One serving = 205 calories
              2 g protein
              33 g carbohydrate
              7 g fat
              203 mg sodium
              231 mg potassium
              0 mg cholesterol

One serving = 1 starch/bread + 1 fruit + 1 fat

*Two cups all-purpose flour plus 1 egg can be substituted by those who do not have food allergies.

Pineapple Upside-Down Cake

½ cup pineapple chunks (packed in
    juice)
¼ cup molasses
½ cup margarine or butter
½ cup honey
1 egg
1½ cups all-purpose flour
1 tablespoon baking powder
¾ cup pineapple juice or water

Preheat the oven to 350°F. Oil bottom of 9-inch square baking pan. Arrange pineapple chunks in bottom of pan. Drizzle molasses over pineapples. Combine margarine, honey, and egg in mixing bowl. Beat well. Add remaining ingredients. Stir until smooth. Pour batter over pineapple chunks. Bake 30–35 minutes or until toothpick inserted into center comes out clean. Let cool 10 minutes in pan before inverting onto serving platter. Cut into 12 squares.

Makes 12 servings

One square = 191 calories
        3 g protein
        37 g carbohydrate
        11 g fat
        187 mg sodium
        205 mg potassium
        26 mg cholesterol

One square = 1 starch/bread + 1 fruit + 2 fats

Banana Spice Cake

1/3 cup vegetable oil
1/3 cup honey
1 ripe banana, chopped fine
1 egg
2 cups all-purpose flour
2 teaspoons baking powder
1/2 teaspoon ground cinnamon
1/4 teaspoon ground nutmeg
1 cup water
1/2 cup chopped walnuts

Preheat the oven to 350°F. Cream together oil, honey, banana, and egg. Add flour, baking powder, cinnamon, nutmeg, and water. Beat until blended. Pour batter into 8-inch square baking pan. Sprinkle on nuts. Bake 30–35 minutes or until toothpick inserted into center comes out clean. Let cool.

Makes 9 servings

One serving = 264 calories
               3 g protein
               43 g carbohydrate
               12 g fat
               72 mg sodium
               311 mg potassium
               16 mg cholesterol

One serving = 1 starch/bread + 2 fruits + 2 fats

Fruit Cocktail Cake

2 cups all-purpose flour
¾ cup sugar
2 teaspoons baking powder
½ teaspoon ground cardamom
½ teaspoon ground nutmeg
½ cup vegetable oil
2 eggs
1 teaspoon lemon extract
1 16-ounce can fruit cocktail, canned
   in juice, undrained
Confectioners' sugar

Preheat the oven to 350°F. Combine flour, sugar, baking powder, cardamom, and nutmeg in mixing bowl. Stir to blend. Cream together oil, eggs, and lemon. Add to flour mixture. Stir in fruit cocktail and juice. Beat until smooth. Pour batter into lightly oiled 9″ × 13″ baking pan. Bake 35–40 minutes or until toothpick inserted into center comes out clean. Let cool. Cut into 12 squares. Sprinkle on confectioners' sugar just before serving.

Makes 12 servings

One square = 184 calories
            2 g protein
            44 g carbohydrate
            7 g fat
            97 mg sodium
            118 mg potassium
            34 mg cholesterol

One square = 1 starch/bread + 2 fruits + 1 fat

German Chocolate Cake

CAKE

> 4 ounces German sweet chocolate
> ½ cup water
> 2 cups all-purpose flour
> 1 tablespoon baking powder
> 1 cup sugar
> 1 4-ounce jar strained baby food
>   prunes
> 1 cup skim milk
> 6 eggs, separated

FROSTING

> ⅓ cup sugar
> 1 tablespoon cornstarch
> 2 tablespoons butter or margarine
> ¾ cup evaporated skim milk
> ½ cup shredded coconut
> ½ cup toasted chopped pecans

Preheat the oven to 350°F. Combine chocolate and water in small saucepan and melt over warm heat about 3 minutes. Let cool. Stir together flour and baking powder. Cream together 1 cup sugar, prunes, milk, egg yolks, and chocolate mixture. Beat egg whites on medium speed of electric mixer until soft peaks form. Fold egg whites into chocolate mixture. Slowly add flour mixture, ¼ cup at a time, folding in with scraper or spatula until smooth. Pour batter into lightly oiled 13″ × 9″ × 2″ baking pan. Bake 20–25 minutes or until toothpick inserted into center comes out clean. Let cool thoroughly.

Make frosting by combining the ⅓ cup sugar, cornstarch, butter, and milk in a saucepan. Cook over medium heat, stirring constantly, until bubbling. Add coconut and pecans. Let cool before spreading over cake.

Makes 24 servings

One serving = 221 calories
　　　　　　　　3 g protein
　　　　　　　　29 g carbohydrate
　　　　　　　　5 g fat
　　　　　　　　89 mg sodium
　　　　　　　　503 mg potassium
　　　　　　　　6 mg cholesterol

One serving = 1 starch/bread + 2 fruits + 1 fat

Yogurt Streusel Coffee Cake

½ cup margarine or butter
½ cup sugar
2 eggs
1 cup vanilla yogurt
½ teaspoon almond extract
(optional)
2 cups all-purpose flour plus
2 teaspoons
1 teaspoon baking powder
½ teaspoon salt
⅓ cup brown sugar, packed
1 teaspoon ground cinnamon
¼ cup chopped pecans
1 tablespoon margarine or butter,
softened

Preheat the oven to 350°F. Cream together margarine, ½ cup sugar, and eggs. Add yogurt and almond extract. Beat 1 minute or until fluffy. Add 2 cups flour, baking powder, and salt. Beat 2 minutes to blend well. Prepare streusel by mixing remaining ingredients in bowl. Pour half of batter in lightly oiled and floured 10-inch tube pan. Sprinkle on half of streusel mixture. Pour remaining batter on top and sprinkle with remaining streusel. Bake 30–40 minutes or until toothpick inserted into center comes out clean. Let cool in pan 5 minutes before inverting to cool.

Makes 15 servings

One serving = 162 calories
                2 g protein
                29 g carbohydrate
                6 g fat
                203 mg sodium
                294 mg potassium
                38 mg cholesterol (margarine)

One serving = 1 starch/bread + 1 fruit + 1 fat

Pumpkin Cream Roll

4 eggs, separated
½ cup sugar
½ cup canned pumpkin
¾ cup all-purpose flour
1 teaspoon baking powder
1 teaspoon ground cinnamon
¼ teaspoon ground nutmeg
⅛ teaspoon ground ginger
Confectioners' sugar
8-ounce package low-fat cream
*   cheese, softened*

Preheat the oven to 400°F. Beat egg yolks on high speed until thick and lemon-colored. Add sugar gradually and beat until foamy. Stir in pumpkin. Beat egg whites until soft peaks form. Fold into egg yolk mixture. Combine flour, baking powder, cinnamon, nutmeg, and ginger in bowl. Stir to blend. Fold into pumpkin mixture. Pour batter into waxed paper–lined 10½″ × 15½″ × 1″ baking pan. Bake 10–12 minutes, or until toothpick inserted into center comes out clean. Loosen edges of cake and turn onto large kitchen towel dusted lightly with confectioners' sugar. Remove waxed paper. Roll cake and towel up in jelly-roll fashion. Let cool completely. Beat cream cheese until soft and creamy. Unroll cake; remove towel. Spread with cream cheese and roll up cake tightly. Sprinkle with confectioners' sugar just before serving.

Makes 16 servings

One serving = 194 calories
     2 g protein
     33 g carbohydrate
     8 g fat
     210 mg sodium
     301 mg potassium
     69 mg cholesterol

One serving = 1 starch/bread + 1 fruit + 1 fat

Chocolate Zucchini Cake

½ cup margarine or butter
1 cup sugar
2 eggs
2 cups all-purpose flour
¼ cup cocoa
1½ teaspoons baking powder
½ teaspoon baking soda
½ teaspoon ground cinnamon
½ cup milk
2 cups grated zucchini
⅓ cup chopped walnuts

Preheat the oven to 350°F. Cream together margarine, sugar, and eggs. Combine flour, cocoa, baking powder, baking soda, and cinnamon. Stir into creamed mixture alternatively with milk. Add zucchini and beat until blended. Pour into lightly oiled 13″ × 9″ baking pan. Sprinkle nuts on top. Bake 35–40 minutes or until cake springs back when touched.

Makes 15 servings

One serving = 247 calories
3 g protein
36 g carbohydrate
13 g fat
233 mg sodium
391 mg potassium
47 mg cholesterol

One serving = 1 starch/bread + 1 fruit + 2 fats

Blueberry-Tofu Pie

2 cups fresh or frozen blueberries*
1/4 cup sugar plus 2 tablespoons
1 tablespoon cornstarch
2 tablespoons orange juice or water
1 10½-ounce package extra-firm tofu
1/4 teaspoon almond extract
1 8-inch prepared graham cracker
    crust

Combine blueberries, ¼ cup sugar, the cornstarch, and orange juice in saucepan. Stir constantly over medium heat while bringing to boil. Boil 1 minute. Remove from heat and let cool. Drain tofu and wrap in paper towel to squeeze out excess water. Puree tofu in blender or food processor with almond extract and remaining 2 tablespoons sugar. Process until smooth. Spread into bottom of graham cracker crust. Pour cooled blueberry mixture over tofu filling. Chill.

Makes 8 servings

One serving = 216 calories
            3 g protein
            34 g carbohydrate
            5 g fat
            97 mg sodium
            208 mg potassium
            0 mg cholesterol

One serving = 1 medium-fat protein + 1 starch/bread
            + 2 fruits + 1 fat

*Strawberries may be substituted for blueberries.

Baked Rice Pudding

1 cup cooked brown rice (⅓ cup
        uncooked)
1 teaspoon vanilla extract
¼ cup raisins
2 cups low-fat milk
2 tablespoons sugar
2 eggs

Preheat the oven to 325°F. Combine all ingredients in bowl. Pour into lightly oiled casserole. Bake 45–50 minutes or until knife inserted into center comes out clean.

Makes 4 servings

One serving = 132 calories
                2 g protein
                27 g carbohydrate
                2 g fat
                189 mg sodium
                234 mg potassium
                41 mg cholesterol

One serving = 1 starch/bread + ½ low-fat milk

Baked Date Pudding

⅔ cup all-purpose flour
¼ cup sugar
2 teaspoons baking powder
2 eggs
½ cup pitted finely chopped dates
½ cup chopped walnuts
½ cup applesauce
½ teaspoon grated orange zest or
     ¼ teaspoon orange extract

Preheat the oven to 350°F. Combine all ingredients in mixing bowl. Beat together thoroughly. Pour batter into well-oiled 8-inch square or round baking pan. Bake 30–40 minutes or until toothpick inserted into center comes out clean. Let cool and cut into slices or squares.

Makes 8 servings

One serving = 164 calories
              2 g protein
              30 g carbohydrate
              4 g fat
              192 mg sodium
              241 mg potassium
              45 mg cholesterol

One serving = 1 starch/bread + 1 fruit + 1 fat

B r o w n i e s

½ cup sugar
½ cup cocoa
⅔ cup soft margarine or butter
2 eggs
¾ cup all-purpose flour
2 teaspoons baking powder
⅓ cup chopped walnuts

Preheat the oven to 350°F. Cream together sugar, cocoa, margarine, and eggs. Add remaining ingredients. Mix well. Pour batter into lightly oiled 8-inch square baking pan. Bake 20–25 minutes or until toothpick inserted into center comes out clean. Cut into 24 squares.

Makes 24 servings

One square = 101 calories
            2 g protein
            23 g carbohydrate
            8 g fat
            127 g sodium
            282 mg potassium
            27 mg cholesterol

One square = 1 starch/bread + 1 fat

Blonde Brownies

⅔ *cup sugar*
½ *cup soft margarine or butter*
1 *egg*
¾ *cup all-purpose flour*
2 *teaspoons baking powder*
½ *teaspoon vanilla extract*
¼ *cup white chocolate chips*

Preheat the oven to 350°F. Beat together sugar, margarine, and egg. Add remaining ingredients. Stir until smooth. Pour batter into lightly oiled 8-inch square baking pan. Bake 20–25 minutes or until golden brown. Cut into 24 squares.

Makes 24 servings

One square = 92 calories
2 g protein
21 g carbohydrate
6 g fat
117 mg sodium
124 mg potassium
23 mg cholesterol

One square = 1 starch/bread + 1 fat

Rice-Flour Brownies

2 squares unsweetened baking chocolate
¼ cup vegetable oil
½ cup sugar
1 cup rice flour*
1 teaspoon baking powder
2 tablespoons tapioca or potato starch*
¼ teaspoon salt
1 teaspoon vanilla extract
½ cup water
½ cup chopped walnuts

Preheat the oven to 350°F. Melt chocolate, oil, and sugar in saucepan over low heat. Let cool. Combine flour, baking powder, starch, and salt. Add chocolate mixture, vanilla, water, and walnuts. Pour into an 8-inch square baking pan. Bake 25–30 minutes or until toothpick inserted into center comes out clean. Let cool. Cut into squares.

Makes 16 brownies

One brownie = 210 calories
              2 g protein
              29 g carbohydrate
              8 g fat
              204 mg sodium
              341 mg potassium
              0 mg cholesterol

One brownie = 1 starch/bread + 1 fat + 1 fruit

---

*One cup all-purpose flour can be substituted for the rice flour and 1 egg can be substituted for the tapioca starch by those who are not allergic to wheat and egg.

Monkey Bars

1¼ *cups all-purpose flour*
2 *teaspoons baking powder*
2 *medium-ripe bananas, mashed*
⅓ *cup packed brown sugar*
1 *egg*
2 *tablespoons vegetable oil*
¼ *teaspoon ground nutmeg*
½ *cup chopped walnuts*
Confectioners' sugar

Preheat the oven to 350°F. Combine flour and baking powder in mixing bowl. Add remaining ingredients except walnuts and the confectioners' sugar and beat thoroughly. Fold in walnuts. Spread batter evenly into lightly oiled 9-inch square baking pan. Bake 20–25 minutes or until wooden pick inserted into center comes out clean. Cool on wire rack. Cut into 18 bars. Sprinkle lightly with confectioners' sugar.

Makes 18 servings

One bar = 206 calories
        2 g protein
        41 g carbohydrate
        8 g fat
        216 mg sodium
        408 mg potassium
        21 mg cholesterol

One bar = 1 starch/bread + 1 fruit + 1 fat

Chocolate–Peanut Butter Treats

*1 1.4-ounce package sugar-free instant
chocolate pudding
½ cup smooth peanut butter
48 graham cracker squares*

Prepare pudding according to package directions. Stir in peanut butter after pudding is thoroughly mixed. Spoon heaping teaspoon of pudding mixture onto each of 24 graham cracker squares. Top with other graham cracker squares to make sandwiches. Place each sandwich on cookie sheet and cover loosely with waxed paper. Freeze. When firm, wrap each sandwich individually in waxed paper. Place in plastic bag or freezer container. Freeze until ready to eat. Remove from freezer 5 minutes before eating.

Makes 24 sandwiches

One serving = 119 calories
                3 g protein
                18 g carbohydrate
                2 g fat
                129 mg sodium
                211 mg potassium
                15 mg cholesterol

One serving = 1 starch/bread

L e m o n   B a r s

1¾ *cups all-purpose flour*
½ *cup rolled oats*
¾ *cup soft margarine or butter*
¼ *cup sugar*
4 *eggs*
¾ *cup sugar*
1 *teaspoon baking powder*
3 *tablespoons lemon juice*
Grated lemon zest
Confectioners' sugar

Preheat the oven to 350°F. Mix together 1½ cups flour, the oats, margarine, and ¼ cup sugar with pastry blender or fork until crumbly. Pat mixture into bottom of 9″ × 13″ baking pan. Bake 20 minutes. Meanwhile, beat eggs until light and fluffy. Add ¾ cup sugar, remaining ¼ cup flour, the baking powder, lemon juice, and lemon zest. Stir to blend. Pour over crust. Bake 20–25 minutes longer or until brown and center is set. Let cool. Cut into bars. Sprinkle with confectioners' sugar just before serving, if desired.

Makes 48 bars

One bar = 167 calories
          4 g protein
          31 g carbohydrate
          8 g fat
          157 mg sodium
          204 mg potassium
          43 mg cholesterol

One bar = 1 starch/bread + 1 fruit + 1 fat

Banana S'mores

8 graham cracker squares
1 medium ripe banana, cut into
       16 slices
12 miniature marshmallows
1 tablespoon chocolate baking chips

Top 4 graham cracker squares with 4 slices of banana on each. Arrange 3 marshmallows on each of the 4 graham cracker squares. Divide chips among graham cracker squares. Top with remaining 4 graham cracker squares. Microwave 20–30 seconds or until marshmallows puff. Serve immediately.

Makes 4 servings

One serving = 98 calories
           2 g protein
           24 g carbohydrate
           3 g fat
           99 mg sodium
           161 mg potassium
           0 mg cholesterol

One serving = 1 starch/bread + 1 fruit

Breakfast Bars

1 cup bran flakes cereal
½ cup raisins
½ cup skim milk
½ cup margarine or butter
½ cup sugar
2 eggs
1 cup all-purpose flour
½ teaspoon baking soda
½ teaspoon ground cinnamon
¼ teaspoon ground allspice

Preheat the oven to 350°F. Soak bran flakes and raisins in milk. Cream together margarine, sugar, and eggs. Beat well. Add flour, baking soda, cinnamon, allspice, and cereal mixture. Mix thoroughly. Pour batter into lightly oiled 8-inch square baking pan. Bake 25–30 minutes or until toothpick inserted into center comes out clean. Remove from oven and cut into 8 squares.

Makes 8 servings

One square = 174 calories
        2 g protein
        31 g carbohydrate
        7 g fat
        184 mg sodium
        291 mg potassium
        36 mg cholesterol

One square = 1 starch/bread + 1 fat + 1 fruit

White Chocolate Nut Crisps

½ cup margarine or butter
¾ cup sugar
1 egg
½ teaspoon grated orange zest
2 cups all-purpose flour
2 teaspoons baking powder
½ cup finely chopped walnuts
½ cup white chocolate chips

Preheat the oven to 375°F. Cream together margarine, sugar, egg, and orange zest. Stir in remaining ingredients. Mix well. Spoon onto lightly oiled baking sheet. Bake 10–12 minutes or until light brown.

Makes 36 cookies

One cookie = 132 calories
        2 g protein
        24 g carbohydrate
        13 g fat
        84 mg sodium
        183 mg potassium
        7 mg cholesterol

One cookie = 1 starch/bread + 1 fat

Teff Chocolate Chip Cookies

1½ cups teff flour*
½ cup tapioca flour*
¾ cup sugar
1 tablespoon baking powder
½ cup water
⅓ cup vegetable oil
½ cup chocolate chips
½ cup chopped walnuts

Preheat the oven to 375°F. Combine all ingredients in mixing bowl. Mix well. Drop dough by spoonfuls onto lightly oiled baking sheet. Bake 10–15 minutes or until brown.

Makes 24 cookies

One cookie = 203 calories
3 g protein
34 g carbohydrate
8 g fat
187 mg sodium
249 mg potassium
0 mg cholesterol

One cookie = 1 starch/bread + 1 fruit + 1 fat

*Two cups all-purpose flour plus 1 egg can be substituted by those who do not have food allergies.

Peanut Butter Cookies

½ cup peanut butter
½ cup soft margarine or butter
½ cup brown sugar, packed
1 egg
1½ cups all-purpose flour
2 teaspoons baking powder

Preheat the oven to 350°F. Cream together peanut butter, margarine, brown sugar, and egg. Add flour and baking powder. Beat well. Shape into 36 2-inch-diameter balls and place on lightly oiled baking sheet. Flatten with fork or bottom of a glass. Bake 10–12 minutes or until brown.

Makes 36 cookies

One cookie = 99 calories
                3 g protein
                19 g carbohydrate
                8 g fat
                94 mg sodium
                87 mg potassium
                11 mg cholesterol

One cookie = 1 starch/bread + 1 fat

Tofu-Spice Cookies

¾ cup vegetable oil
⅔ cup honey
2 eggs
12 ounces soft tofu
2¼ cups whole-wheat flour
2 teaspoons ground ginger
1 teaspoon ground cinnamon
1 teaspoon ground nutmeg
1 teaspoon baking soda
1 cup raisins
½ cup chopped walnuts
1 cup chopped dates

Preheat the oven to 350°F. Combine oil, honey, eggs, and tofu in blender or mixing bowl. Mix until smooth. Add remaining ingredients. Beat well. Drop by teaspoonfuls on lightly oiled baking pan. Bake 15–20 minutes or until lightly brown.

Makes 48 cookies

One cookie = 301 calories
          8 g protein
          52 g carbohydrate
          13 g fat
          219 mg sodium
          316 mg potassium
          19 mg cholesterol

One cookie = 2 starches/breads + 1 fruit + 2 fats

Chocolate Chip Bar Cookies

½ cup margarine or butter, softened
½ cup light brown sugar,
  packed firm
1 egg
1 ripe banana, mashed
1½ cups all-purpose flour
½ teaspoon baking soda
½ teaspoon baking powder
½ cup chocolate chips
¼ cup chopped walnuts

Preheat the oven to 350°F. Cream together margarine, brown sugar, egg, and banana until smooth. Add flour, baking soda, and baking powder. Beat well. Stir in chocolate chips and walnuts. Pour batter into lightly oiled 9" × 13" baking pan. Spread dough evenly. Bake for 15 minutes or until brown.

Makes 30 squares

One square = 265 calories
              2 g protein
              33 g carbohydrate
              13 g fat
              199 mg sodium
              284 mg potassium
              12 mg cholesterol (margarine)

One square = 1 starch/bread + 1 fruit + 2 fats

Rice Flour–Chocolate Chip Cookies

⅓ *cup sugar*
⅓ *cup vegetable oil*
1 *egg*
¾ *cup rice flour**
2 *tablespoons potato starch**
2 *teaspoons baking powder*
1 *teaspoon vanilla*
½ *cup chocolate chips*

Preheat the oven to 350°F. Cream together sugar, oil, and egg. Add rice flour, potato starch, baking powder, and vanilla. Beat in chocolate chips. Drop onto lightly oiled baking sheet. Bake 10–12 minutes or until browned around edges.

Makes 18 cookies.

One cookie = 241 calories
          2 g protein
          32 g carbohydrate
          13 g fat
          219 mg sodium
          291 mg potassium
          24 mg cholesterol

One cookie = 1 starch/bread + 2 fats + 1 fruit

*One cup all-purpose flour can be substituted by those who do not have food allergies.

Chocolate Tea Cookies

½ cup margarine or butter
½ cup sugar
1 egg
1¼ cups all-purpose flour
½ teaspoon baking powder
1 tablespoon cocoa

Preheat the oven to 350°F. Cream together margarine, sugar, and egg. Combine remaining ingredients in mixing bowl. Stir to mix. Add flour mixture to creamed mixture using low speed on mixer or by hand. Chill dough thoroughly, at least 3 hours. Place dough into cookie press.* Shape dough into desired forms on ungreased baking sheet. Bake 7–10 minutes or until light brown on the edges.

Makes 36 cookies

One cookie = 161 calories
               2 g protein
               31 g carbohydrate
               7 g fat
               121 mg sodium
               199 mg potassium
               14 mg cholesterol

One cookie = 1 starch/bread + 1 fruit + 1 fat

*If cookie press is not available, drop dough by teaspoonfuls onto ungreased cookie sheet. Flatten with a glass.

Oatmeal Cookies

1 cup vegetable oil
¾ cup packed light brown sugar
1½ cups rolled oats
2 cups rice flour*
1 tablespoon baking powder
1½ teaspoons ground cinnamon
½ teaspoon ground nutmeg
¾ cup applesauce
½ cup raisins
¾ cup chopped nuts

Preheat the oven to 375°F. Combine all ingredients in mixing bowl. Beat together well. Drop by teaspoonfuls onto lightly oiled baking sheet. Bake 10–15 minutes or until brown.

Makes 48 cookies

One cookie = 186 calories
　　　　　　2 g protein
　　　　　　32 g carbohydrate
　　　　　　12 g fat
　　　　　　197 mg sodium
　　　　　　274 mg potassium
　　　　　　0 mg cholesterol

One cookie = 1 starch/bread + 1 fruit + 2 fats

*Two cups all-purpose flour can be substituted by those who are not allergic to wheat.

Snickerdoodles

½ cup margarine or butter
½ cup sugar plus 2 tablespoons
1 egg
1½ cups all-purpose flour
¼ teaspoon salt
½ teaspoon baking soda
1 teaspoon ground cinnamon

Preheat the oven to 375°F. Cream together margarine, ½ cup sugar, and egg. Add flour, salt, baking soda, and ½ teaspoon of the ground cinnamon. Mix well. Combine remaining 2 table-spoons sugar and cinnamon in small bowl. Pinch off portions of dough to make 36 walnut-size balls. Roll each ball in cinnamon-sugar mixture. Place on lightly oiled baking sheet. Flatten with bottom of glass. Bake 8–10 minutes or until light brown.

Makes 36 cookies

One cookie = 118 calories
          2 g protein
          21 g carbohydrate
          8 g fat
          169 mg sodium
          201 mg potassium
          21 mg cholesterol (margarine)

One cookie = 1 starch/bread + 1 fat

Hermits

½ *cup brown sugar*
½ *cup margarine or butter*
1 *egg*
1⅓ *cups all-purpose flour*
¾ *teaspoon ground cinnamon*
½ *teaspoon baking soda*
¼ *teaspoon ground cloves*
½ *cup currants*
½ *cup chopped dried apricots*
½ *cup low-fat plain yogurt*

Preheat the oven to 375°F. Cream together sugar, margarine, and egg until light and fluffy. Add remaining ingredients. Beat until well blended. Drop by teaspoonfuls onto lightly oiled baking pan. Bake 12–15 minutes or until brown on edges.

Makes 36 cookies

One cookie = 233 calories
2 g protein
41 g carbohydrate
7 g fat
192 mg sodium
304 mg potassium
27 mg cholesterol (margarine)

One cookie = 1 starch/bread + 2 fruits + 1 fat

Crunchy Rice Granola

1 cup cooked brown rice
1 cup natural, unsalted peanuts
1 cup shredded coconut
2 tablespoons sesame seeds
1 cup chopped walnuts
¼ cup soy milk or apple juice
½ cup Cream of Rice cereal,
    uncooked
⅓ cup brown sugar
¼ cup vegetable oil

Preheat the oven to 250°F. Combine all ingredients, except oil, on baking sheet and mix with wooden spoon. Pour oil over mixture and toss lightly. Bake 1½ hours or until mixture is brown and dried. Stir mixture every 10–15 minutes during baking to toast evenly. Pour into sealed container. Use as cereal or snack. This cereal can be stored on the pantry shelf if used within 2 to 3 weeks.

Makes 4 cups

One serving of ½ cup = 224 calories
                  2 g protein
                  31 g carbohydrate
                  14 g fat
                  202 mg sodium
                  291 mg potassium
                  0 mg cholesterol

One serving = 1 starch/bread + 1 fruit + 2 fats

Amaranth Granola

1 cup amaranth flour*
2 tablespoons carob powder
½ cup coarsely chopped pecans or
    other nuts (optional)
2 to 3 tablespoons sesame seeds
¼ teaspoon salt (optional)
2 tablespoons oil
2 to 4 tablespoons maple syrup or
    molasses
3 to 4 tablespoons boiling water

Preheat the oven to 250°F. Mix amaranth, carob, pecans, sesame seeds, and salt in mixing bowl. In small bowl or cup, mix oil, maple syrup, and boiling water. Stir rapidly, pour over dry ingredients and mix well. Crumble lumps. Cut through mixture several times with table knife until particles are about the size of peas. Spread evenly on baking sheet with edges. Bake for 30 minutes. Remove from oven and stir. Turn off oven and let granola cool in oven. Store in tightly closed jar.

Makes 2 cups

One serving of ½ cup = 159 calories
                3 g protein
                22 g carbohydrate
                7 g fat
                229 mg sodium
                194 mg potassium
                0 mg cholesterol

One serving = 1 starch/bread + 1 fat

*One cup oatmeal can be substituted by those who do not have food allergies.

Apple Crisp

4 cups sliced, peeled apples
1/2 cup apple juice
1 tablespoon tapioca or 2 tablespoons
    all-purpose flour
1/2 cup oatmeal
1/4 cup flour
1/3 cup chopped walnuts
1 teaspoon ground cinnamon
1/4 teaspoon ground nutmeg
1/4 cup melted margarine or butter
2 tablespoons honey

Preheat the oven to 350°F. Place apple slices in lightly oiled 8-inch square baking pan. Pour apple juice over apple slices. Sprinkle on tapioca. Combine remaining ingredients in mixing bowl. Toss together until crumbly. Scatter oatmeal mixture over apples. Bake 20–25 minutes or until apples are tender. Let cool 10 minutes before serving.

Makes 4 servings

One serving = 203 calories
           3 g protein
           44 g carbohydrate
           7 g fat
           96 mg sodium
           289 mg potassium
           0 mg cholesterol

One serving = 2 fruits + 1 starch/bread + 1 fat

Amaranth Apple Crisp

3 cups sliced apples
¼ cup apple juice
1 tablespoon honey
*2 tablespoons soy flour**
*¼ cup amaranth flour**
½ teaspoon cinnamon
2 tablespoons vegetable oil

Preheat the oven to 350°F. Put apple slices in lightly oiled baking pan. Pour on apple juice. Drizzle honey over apples. Combine soy and amaranth flours and cinammon in mixing bowl. Add vegetable oil and toss lightly. Sprinkle crumbly mixture over apples. Bake 20 minutes or until lightly brown.

Makes 4 servings

One serving = 261 calories
2 g protein
43 g carbohydrate
8 g fat
184 mg sodium
304 mg potassium
0 mg cholesterol

One serving = 2 fruits + 1 starch/bread + 1 fat

*One-third cup all-purpose flour can be substituted by those who do not have food allergies.

Apple Tart with Cheddar Topping

3 medium baking apples, peeled and
    cored
1 9-inch prepared piecrust
2 egg whites
¾ cup low-fat vanilla yogurt
1 cup (8 ounces) shredded cheddar
    cheese
2 tablespoons sugar
½ teaspoon ground cinnamon
¼ teaspoon ground nutmeg
2 tablespoons all-purpose flour

Preheat the oven to 375°F. Thinly slice apples and arrange evenly over bottom of piecrust. In mixing bowl, combine remaining ingredients. Beat with wire whisk until smooth. Pour over apples. Bake 40–45 minutes or until topping is firm and brown. Let cool on wire rack. Serve warm.

Makes 8 servings

One serving = 317 calories
         9 g protein
         42 g carbohydrate
         8 g fat
         419 mg sodium
         386 mg potassium
         89 mg cholesterol

One serving = 1 starch/bread + 1 high-fat protein + 2 fruits
        + 1 fat

F r o z e n   F r u i t   D e l i g h t

1 0.3-*ounce package orange-flavored
     gelatin*
1 *cup vanilla-flavored frozen yogurt*
1 8-*ounce can juice-packed crushed
     pineapple, drained*
1 *banana, peeled and diced*
1 11-*ounce can mandarin oranges in
     light syrup*
¼ *cup chopped pecans*

Prepare gelatin according to package directions, except use ½ cup less cold water. Let cool until mixture coats a spoon. Soften frozen yogurt until it is the consistency of whipped topping. Fold into gelatin. Add fruit and pecans to mixture. Pour into mold or serving bowl. Freeze overnight or at least 4 hours. Remove from freezer 5–10 minutes before serving.

Makes 6 servings

One serving = 151 calories
              1 g protein
              26 g carbohydrate
              6 g fat
              219 mg sodium
              416 mg potassium
              4 mg cholesterol

One serving = 2 fruits + 1 fat

Fruit Kabobs with Chocolate Dip

24 fresh strawberries, stems removed
12 pineapple chunks (juice-packed or
    fresh)
2 kiwifruit, peeled and cut into 12
    chunks
24 chunks honeydew or cantaloupe
½ cup cocoa powder
¼ cup hot water
½ cup sweetened condensed canned
    skim milk

Arrange fruit on serving tray or thread onto skewers. Combine cocoa powder and hot water in bowl and beat until smooth. Add milk. Heat over low heat, stirring constantly, until warm. Serve chocolate dip with fruit.

Makes 6 servings

One serving = 168 calories
               1 g protein
               25 g carbohydrate
               0 g fat
               161 mg sodium
               518 mg potassium
               2 mg cholesterol

One serving = 2 fruits

Strawberry Smoothie

½ *cup sliced strawberries*
½ *cup vanilla yogurt*
½ *banana*

Process all ingredients in blender until combined and smooth. Serve immediately.

Makes 1 serving

One serving = 164 calories
5 g protein
342 g carbohydrate
1 g fat
99 mg sodium
312 mg potassium
2 mg cholesterol

One serving = 1 low-fat milk + 1 fruit

Bran Muffin Classic

1 cup whole-wheat flour
1 cup bran cereal
2 teaspoons baking powder
1 egg or egg substitute
2 tablespoons sugar or molasses
2 tablespoons vegetable oil
¾ cup water
¼ cup raisins

Preheat the oven to 400°F. Combine all ingredients in mixing bowl. Beat just until flour is moistened. Spoon into lightly oiled or paper-lined muffin cups. Bake 15–18 minutes. Cool.

Makes 9 muffins

One muffin = 109 calories
              3 g protein
              16 g carbohydrate
              5 g fat
              171 mg sodium
              189 mg potassium
              36 mg cholesterol

One muffin = 1 starch/bread + 1 fat

Orange Quinoa Muffins

3⅔ cups (1 pound) quinoa flour*
1 teaspoon baking soda
½ teaspoon salt
Grated zest of 2 oranges
Juice of 2 oranges
¼ cup vegetable oil
½ cup maple syrup
¾ cup water

Preheat the oven to 375°F. Stir flour, soda, and salt together. Add orange zest and juice of oranges. Stir in oil, syrup, and water. Spoon batter into muffin cups. Bake 18–22 minutes or until toothpick inserted into center comes out clean.

Makes 12 muffins

One muffin = 191 calories
            2 g protein
            27 g carbohydrate
            7 g fat
            189 mg sodium
            240 mg potassium
            o mg cholesterol

One muffin = 1 starch/bread + 1 fat + 1 fruit

*Two cups all-purpose flour plus 1 egg can be substituted by those who do not have food allergies.

Apple-Cinnamon Muffins

2 cups all-purpose flour
1 tablespoon baking powder
1 tablespoon sugar
1 teaspoon ground cinnamon
1 egg
2 tablespoons vegetable oil
¾ cup skim milk
½ cup unsweetened applesauce
¼ cup raisins

Preheat the oven to 375°F. Combine all ingredients in mixing bowl. Beat just until mixed. Spoon batter into lightly oiled muffin cups or paper-lined muffin cups. Bake 20–25 minutes or until brown.

Makes 12 muffins

One muffin = 137 calories
            3 g protein
            26 g carbohydrate
            6 g fat
            56 mg sodium
            141 mg potassium
            61 mg cholesterol

One muffin = 1 starch/bread + 1 fat

Teff Banana Muffins

2½ cups teff flour*
1½ tablespoons baking powder
½ cup sugar
1 teaspoon ground cinnamon
1½ cups water
¼ cup vegetable oil
2 bananas
1 egg

Preheat the oven to 400°F. Combine flour, baking powder, sugar, and cinnamon in mixing bowl. Puree water, oil, bananas, and egg in blender or food processor. Add to dry ingredients. Mix well. Spoon batter into muffin cups. Bake 10–15 minutes or until toothpick inserted into center comes out clean.

Makes 12 muffins

One muffin = 192 calories
            4 g protein
            34 g carbohydrate
            8 g fat
            194 mg sodium
            304 mg potassium
            22 mg cholesterol

One muffin = 1 starch/bread + 1 fruit + 1 fat

*Two-and-a-half cups all-purpose flour can be substituted by those who do not have food allergies.

Corn Muffins or Cornbread

2 cups cornmeal
1 tablespoon baking powder
1 tablespoon sugar
¼ teaspoon salt
2 eggs
2 tablespoons vegetable oil
¾ cup water

Preheat the oven to 400°F. Combine all ingredients in mixing bowl. Beat to blend. Pour into lightly oiled muffin tins or 8-inch square baking pan. Bake 15–20 minutes or until golden brown.

Makes 9 muffins or squares

One serving = 95 calories
            2 g protein
            23 g carbohydrate
            9 g fat
            219 mg sodium
            198 mg potassium
            27 mg cholesterol

One serving = 1 starch/bread + 1 fat

Rice Flour Muffins

1 cup rice flour*
1 teaspoon xanthan gum*
¼ teaspoon salt (optional)
2 teaspoons baking powder
1 tablespoon honey
⅔ cup water
2 tablespoons vegetable oil
½ cup diced fruit or berries
     (optional)

Preheat the oven to 375°F. Combine rice flour, xanthan gum, salt, and baking powder in mixing bowl. Stir to blend ingredients. Add honey, water, and oil. Pour batter into greased muffin tins. Bake 12–15 minutes or until toothpick inserted into center comes out clean.

Makes 6 muffins

One muffin = 171 calories
                2 g protein
                32 g carbohydrate
                7 g fat
                203 mg sodium
                217 mg potassium
                0 mg cholesterol

One muffin = 1 starch/bread + 1 fruit + 1 fat

*One cup all-purpose flour + 1 egg can be substituted by those who do not have food allergies.

Banana Bread

⅓ cup vegetable oil
⅔ cup sugar
2 eggs
2 ripe bananas, chopped
1 cup all-purpose flour
½ cup soy flour*
2 teaspoons baking powder
½ teaspoon salt
¼ teaspoon ground mace or nutmeg
¼ cup skim milk or water

Preheat the oven to 350°F. Puree oil, sugar, eggs, and bananas in blender or food processor until smooth. Combine flours, baking powder, salt, and mace in mixing bowl. Stir to blend. Add banana mixture and milk. Beat until smooth. Pour batter into lightly oiled 9" × 5" loaf pan. Bake 40–45 minutes or until center springs back to touch. Remove from pan and let cool on wire rack.

Makes 12 servings

One serving of 1 slice = 162 calories
                        5 g protein
                        34 g carbohydrate
                        6 g fat
                        106 mg sodium
                        301 mg potassium
                        0 mg cholesterol

One serving = 1 starch/bread + 2 fruits + 1 fat

---

*All-purpose flour can be substituted. The protein content is less if soy flour is not used.

Spelt Biscuits

2 cups spelt flour*
1½ tablespoons baking powder
½ teaspoon salt
¼ cup vegetable oil
¾ cup cold water

Preheat the oven to 425°F. Combine all ingredients in mixing bowl. Beat well. Drop by spoonfuls onto baking pan. Bake 10–12 minutes or until brown on bottom.

Makes 12 biscuits

One biscuit = 119 calories
                    2 g protein
                    23 g carbohydrate
                    7 g fat
                    204 mg sodium
                    181 mg potassium
                    0 mg cholesterol

One biscuit = 1 starch/bread + 1 fat

---

*Two cups all-purpose flour can be substituted for those who do not have food allergies.

HOLIDAY FAVORITES

Herbed Bread Stuffing

4 cups bread cubes
1 cup chopped celery
⅓ cup chopped onion
1 tablespoon chopped fresh parsley
    leaves
1 clove garlic, minced
½ to ¾ cup hot water
½ teaspoon freshly ground black
    pepper
1 teaspoon ground sage
½ teaspoon dried marjoram leaves
½ teaspoon dried thyme leaves
¼ teaspoon dried basil leaves

Preheat the oven to 350°F. Combine all ingredients in mixing bowl. If a moist dressing is desired, use ¾ cup hot water. Toss with wooden spoon. Stuff Cornish hen, chicken, or turkey or bake separately in lightly oiled casserole 30–35 minutes.

Makes 8 servings

One serving of ½ cup = 94 calories
                      3 g protein
                      18 g carbohydrate
                      2 g fat
                      189 mg sodium
                      172 mg potassium
                      0 mg cholesterol

One serving = 1 starch/bread + 1 vegetable

Cranberry–Wild Rice Stuffing

½ cup wild rice, uncooked
¼ cup golden raisins
1 cup water
5 scallions, chopped
½ cup chopped celery or fennel bulb
1 tablespoon vegetable oil
1 cup fresh or frozen cranberries
¼ cup honey
2 teaspoons grated orange zest
1 teaspoon dried thyme leaves

Preheat the oven to 350°F. Cook wild rice and raisins in water over medium heat about 45 minutes or until rice is tender. Drain off any water. Sauté scallions and celery in oil until tender, about 5 minutes. Add cranberries, honey, orange zest, thyme, and rice mixture. Mix well. Stuff into Cornish hens, chicken, or turkey breast. Bake 50–55 minutes or until poultry is done.

Makes 4 servings

One serving of ½ cup = 179 calories
3 g protein
29 g carbohydrate
7 g fat
157 mg sodium
206 mg potassium
0 mg cholesterol

One serving = 1 starch/bread + 1 fruit + 1 fat

Apricot Bread Dressing

1 cup chopped dried apricots
1½ cups water or turkey stock
1 cup chopped celery
½ cup chopped pine nuts or walnuts
12 slices whole-wheat bread, dried
and cut into small cubes

Preheat the oven to 350°F. Cook apricots in water or stock just until boiling. Remove from heat and let stand 10 minutes. Add celery, nuts, and bread. Toss lightly to moisten bread. Spoon into turkey or lightly oiled baking dish with a cover. Bake until turkey is done or 40 minutes if cooked separately. Remove cover during last 10 minutes of baking to brown top, if cooked separately.

Makes 12 servings

One serving of ½ cup = 122 calories
4 g protein
23 g carbohydrate
3 g fat
134 mg sodium
241 mg potassium
0 mg cholesterol

One serving = 1 starch/bread + 1 fruit

Sweet Potatoes à l'Orange

2 pounds sweet potatoes, cooked, or
  2 pounds vacuum-packed
  sweet potatoes
4 teaspoons margarine or butter,
  melted
1 teaspoon ground cinnamon
2 tablespoons frozen orange juice
  concentrate
12 dried apricot halves
Fresh orange slices

Preheat the oven to 425°F. Arrange sweet potatoes in shallow baking dish. Combine margarine, cinnamon, and orange juice concentrate. Pour over potatoes. Arrange apricot halves on top. Bake, covered, 10–15 minutes. Top with orange slices before serving.

Makes 4 servings

One serving = 192 calories
            3 g protein
            29 g carbohydrate
            8 g fat
            91 mg sodium
            497 mg potassium
            0 mg cholesterol

One serving = 1 starch/bread + 1 fruit + 1 fat

Apple-Stuffed Acorn Squash

2 medium acorn squash
1 apple, chopped
1/4 cup raisins
1/4 cup chopped pecans
1 teaspoon ground cinnamon
1 tablespoon honey

Preheat the oven to 400°F. Cut squash in half and remove the seeds. Combine apple, raisins, pecans, and cinnamon in bowl. Stir to mix. Fill squash with mixture. Drizzle honey over squash. Place in baking pan. Cover with lid or foil and bake for 25 minutes. Remove lid and continue to bake 15–20 minutes or until squash is tender.

Makes 4 servings

One serving = 161 calories
            3 g protein
            36 g carbohydrate
            4 g fat
            78 mg sodium
            119 mg potassium
            0 mg cholesterol

One serving = 1 starch/bread + 1 fruit

Christmas Fruitcake Cookies

²⁄₃ *cup vegetable oil*
½ *cup light brown sugar, packed*
1 *egg*
1¼ *cups all-purpose flour*
1 *teaspoon baking powder*
1 *teaspoon ground cinnamon*
½ *teaspoon ground cloves*
¼ *teaspoon ground allspice*
½ *cup skim milk*
½ *cup chopped walnuts*
½ *cup golden raisins*
½ *cup snipped dried apricots*
½ *cup chopped dates*

Preheat the oven to 350°F. Cream together oil, sugar, and egg. Add remaining ingredients. Mix well. Drop by teaspoonfuls onto lightly oiled baking sheet. Bake 10–12 minutes or until browned on edges. Let cool on wire rack and store in tightly closed container.

Makes 36 cookies

One cookie = 97 calories
    2 g protein
    16 g carbohydrate
    6 g fat
    68 mg sodium
    129 mg potassium
    15 mg cholesterol

One cookie = 1 starch/bread + 1 fat

Rolled Sugar Cookies

½ cup margarine or butter, softened
½ cup sugar
1 teaspoon vanilla extract
1 egg
1¾ cups all-purpose flour
2 teaspoons baking powder

Cream together margarine, sugar, vanilla, and egg until light and fluffy. Add flour and baking powder. Beat well. Chill dough for 2 hours or overnight. Preheat the oven to 375°F. Roll out dough onto lightly floured surface until ⅛ inch thick. Cut with cookie cutter. Place on an ungreased baking sheet. Bake about 10 minutes or until light brown. Let cool.

Makes 36 cookies

One cookie = 129 calories
             2 g protein
             19 g carbohydrate
             4 g fat
             107 mg sodium
             39 mg potassium
             27 mg cholesterol

One cookie = 1 starch/bread + 1 fat

R u s s i a n   T e a   C a k e s

1 cup margarine or butter, softened
½ cup confectioners' sugar
1 teaspoon vanilla extract
1½ cups all-purpose flour
½ cup chopped pecans, toasted

Preheat the oven to 375°F. Cream together margarine, sugar, and vanilla until light and fluffy. Mix in flour and pecans. Chill at least 2 hours or overnight. Pinch off small pieces of the dough and roll into 1-inch balls. Place on an ungreased baking sheet. Bake 10–12 minutes or until light brown. Let cool on wire rack. Roll in additional confectioners' sugar before serving. Store in airtight container.

Makes 36 cookies

One cookie = 92 calories
2 g protein
12 g carbohydrate
7 g fat
78 mg sodium
37 mg potassium
0 mg cholesterol

One cookie = 1 starch/bread + 1 fat

Fruitcake

½ *cup chopped dates*
½ *cup chopped dried figs*
½ *cup chopped prunes*
1 *cup crushed pineapple, packed in*
    juice
1 *cup raisins*
1 *medium apple, chopped*
½ *cup chopped walnuts*
½ *cup orange juice*
2 *cups all-purpose flour*
1 *tablespoon baking powder*
1 *teaspoon baking soda*
1 *teaspoon ground cinnamon*
½ *teaspoon ground nutmeg*
2 *eggs*

Preheat the oven to 350°F. Combine dates, figs, prunes, pineapple, raisins, apple, walnuts, and orange juice in mixing bowl. Add remaining ingredients and mix well. Pour into lightly oiled 10-inch tube pan. Bake 40–45 minutes or until toothpick inserted into center comes out clean. Let cool 5 minutes in pan before removing. Cool thoroughly before wrapping in foil.

Makes 15 servings

One serving = 196 calories
            5 g protein
            37 g carbohydrate
            5 g fat
            132 mg sodium
            371 mg potassium
            39 mg cholesterol

One serving = 1 starch/bread + 2 fruits + 1 fat

Pumpkin Pudding Cake

2 cups all-purpose flour
1 cup sugar
1½ teaspoons baking powder
½ teaspoon baking soda
1 teaspoon ground cinnamon
½ teaspoon ground cloves
1 cup cooked or canned pumpkin
½ cup vegetable oil
1 egg
½ cup raisins
½ cup chopped pecans
Confectioners' sugar or vanilla
*   yogurt*

Preheat the oven to 350°F. Combine flour, sugar, baking powder, baking soda, cinnamon, and cloves in mixing bowl. Add pumpkin, oil, and egg. Beat 3 minutes at medium speed until thoroughly mixed. Stir in raisins and pecans. Pour batter into lightly oiled 3-quart ring mold or cheesecake pan. Bake 40–45 minutes or until toothpick inserted into center comes out clean. Let cool 5 minutes before removing from pan. Serve warm with sprinkle of confectioners' sugar or spoonful of vanilla yogurt.

Makes 24 1-inch slices

One serving = 201 calories
        3 g protein
        26 g carbohydrate
        11 g fat
        86 mg sodium
        185 mg potassium
        21 mg cholesterol

One serving = 1 starch/bread + 1 fruit + 2 fats

Chocolate Chip Cheesecake

1½ cups graham cracker crumbs
⅓ cup margarine or butter, melted
2 8-ounce packages low-fat cream
        cheese, softened
6 eggs
½ cup sugar
1 cup plain low-fat yogurt
2 teaspoons vanilla extract
1 cup chocolate baking chips

Preheat the oven to 400°F. Toss graham cracker crumbs and margarine together. Press into bottom of 10-inch springform pan. Set aside. Combine cream cheese, egg yolks, and sugar in food processor or mixing bowl. Beat until smooth. Pour cream-cheese mixture into bowl and stir in yogurt and vanilla. Beat egg whites until soft peaks form. Fold cream-cheese mixture into egg whites. Gently fold in chocolate chips. Pour over crust. Place in oven. Reduce heat to 300°F and bake 1 hour. Turn oven off and let cheesecake bake for 1 hour longer. Let cool 2 hours at room temperature before refrigerating until ready to serve.

Makes 18 servings

One serving = 194 calories
              5 g protein
              26 g carbohydrate
              14 g fat
              159 mg sodium
              176 mg potassium
              97 mg cholesterol

One serving = 1 starch/bread + 1 fruit + 2 fats

Pumpkin Cheesecake

1 cup crushed vanilla wafers (about
    30 cookies)
3 tablespoons margarine or butter
1 8-ounce package low-fat cream
    cheese, softened
1 cup low-fat ricotta cheese
1 cup canned evaporated skim milk
4 eggs, separated
1 cup cooked or canned pumpkin
⅓ cup sugar
1½ teaspoons ground cinnamon
½ teaspoon ground nutmeg
¼ teaspoon ground cloves
2 tablespoons brandy or brandy
    extract

Preheat the oven to 350°F. Combine vanilla wafers and margarine in bowl. Press mixture into bottom of a 10-inch springform pan. Set aside. Beat together cream cheese, ricotta cheese, milk, egg yolks, pumpkin, sugar, cinnamon, nutmeg, cloves, and brandy until light and fluffy. Beat egg whites in separate bowl until soft peaks form. Fold egg whites into pumpkin mixture. Pour batter into pan. Bake 60–70 minutes or until center is set. Let cool on wire rack 1 hour before chilling.

Makes 18 1-inch slices

One serving = 227 calories
              5 g protein
              27 g carbohydrate
              12 g fat
              167 mg sodium
              241 mg potassium
              84 mg cholesterol

One serving = 1 starch/bread + 1 fruit + 2 fats

Cranberry Nut Bread

2 cups all-purpose flour
½ cup sugar
1 tablespoon baking powder
1 tablespoon grated orange zest
1 cup orange juice
3 tablespoons vegetable oil
1 egg
1 cup chopped fresh or frozen
    cranberries
½ cup raisins
½ cup chopped walnuts

Preheat the oven to 350°F. Combine flour, sugar, baking powder, and orange zest in mixing bowl. Add remaining ingredients and stir to blend well. Pour into an oiled 9″ × 5″ loaf pan. Bake for 45 minutes or until toothpick inserted into center comes out clean. Let cool for 5–10 minutes before removing from pan. Cool thoroughly on wire rack. Wrap in foil or waxed paper at least one day before slicing.

Makes 15 servings

One serving = 147 calories
            3 g protein
            28 g carbohydrate
            7 g fat
            82 mg sodium
            241 mg potassium
            26 mg cholesterol

One serving = 1 starch/bread + 1 fruit + 1 fat

APPENDIX

EXCHANGE LIST FOR MEAL PLANNING

Exchange lists have been produced by the American Diabetes Association and the American Dietetic Association to aid in meal planning. Foods are grouped together based on their similarities in carbohydrate, protein, and fat content. Serving sizes for a stated food are indicated.

Some of the foods listed in *Exchange List for Meal Planning* are provided for reference in assessing how these menus and recipes can be used in your diabetic meal plan.

Starch List

Each food in this list contains about 15 grams of carbohydrate, 3 grams of protein, 1 gram or less of fat, and about 80 calories per serving. In general, one starch exchange is:

- ½ cup cereal, pasta, or starchy vegetable
- 1 ounce of a bread product or 1 slice of bread
- ¾ to 1 ounce of most snack foods (some snack foods may have extra fat)

BREADS

Bagel . . . . ½ (1 ounce)
Bread, reduced calorie. . . . . 2 slices
                                            (1½ ounces)
Bread, white, whole wheat,
     pumpernickel, rye . . . . 1 slice (1 ounce)

Bread sticks, crisp,
    4 inches long × ½ inch . . . . 2 (⅔ ounce)
English muffin . . . . ½
Hot dog or hamburger bun . . . . ½ (1 ounce)
Pita, 6 inches across. . . . . ½
Raisin bread, unfrosted . . . . 1 slice (1 ounce)
Roll, plain, small . . . . 1 (1 ounce)
Tortilla, corn, 6 inches across 1
Tortilla, flour, 7–8 inches across 1
Waffle, 4½ inches square, reduced fat 1

CEREALS AND GRAINS

Bran cereals. . . . . ½ cup
Bulgur. . . . . ½ cup
Cereals, cooked. ½ cup
Cereals, unsweetened, ready-to-eat . . . . . . ¾ cup
Cornmeal (dry). 3 tablespoons
Couscous. . . . . ⅓ cup
Flour (dry). . . . . 3 tablespoons
Granola, low-fat. ¼ cup
Grape Nuts . . . . ¼ cup
Grits (cooked) . . . . ½ cup
Kasha . . . . ½ cup
Millet . . . . ¼ cup
Muesli. . . . . ¼ cup
Oats . . . . ½ cup
Pasta . . . . ½ cup
Puffed cereal . . . . 1½ cups
Rice, white or brown (cooked). . . . . ⅓ cup
Rice milk . . . . ½ cup
Shredded wheat. ½ cup
Sugar-frosted cereal . . . . ½ cup
Wheat germ . . . . 3 tablespoons

STARCHY VEGETABLES

Baked beans . . . . ⅓ cup
Corn . . . . ½ cup
Corn on cob, medium . . . . 1 (5 ounces)
Mixed vegetables with
       corn, peas, or pasta . . . . 1 cup
Peas, green . . . . ½ cup
Plantain. . . . . ½ cup
Potato, baked or boiled . . . . 1 small (3 ounces)
Potato, mashed . . . . ½ cup
Squash, winter (acorn, butternut) . . . . 1 cup
Yam, sweet potato, plain . . . . ½ cup

CRACKERS AND SNACKS

Animal crackers. 8
Graham crackers, 2½-inch square 3
Matzo . . . . ¾ ounce
Melba toast . . . . 4 slices
Oyster crackers 24
Popcorn (popped, no fat added
       or low-fat microwave) . . . . 3 cups
Pretzels . . . . ¾ ounce
Rice cakes, 4 inches across. 2
Saltine-type crackers 6
Snack chips, fat-free (tortilla, potato) . . . . . 15–20 (¾ ounce)
Whole-wheat crackers, no fat added. . . . . . 2–5 (¾ ounce)

STARCHY FOODS PREPARED WITH FAT
(COUNT AS 1 STARCH EXCHANGE,
PLUS 1 FAT EXCHANGE)

Biscuit, 2½ inches across 1
Chow mein noodles. . . . . ½ cup
Cornbread, 2-inch cube. . . . . 1 (2 ounces)
Crackers, round butter-type 6
Croutons . . . . 1 cup
French-fried potatoes. . . . . 16–25 (3 ounces)

Granola. . . . . ¼ cup
Muffin, small . . . . 1 (1½ ounces)
Pancake, 4 inches across 2
Popcorn, microwave (fat added). . . . . 3 cups
Sandwich crackers,
        cheese or peanut butter filling 3
Stuffing, bread (prepared) . . . . ⅓ cup
Taco shell, 6 inches across 2
Waffle, 4½-inch square 1
Whole-wheat crackers, fat added . . . . 4–6 (1 ounce)

Fruit List

Each food in this list contains about 15 grams of carbohydrate and
60 calories per serving. In general, one fruit exchange is:

- 1 small to medium fresh fruit
- ½ cup canned or fresh fruit or fruit juice
- ¼ cup dried fruit

FRUIT

Apple, unpeeled, small . . . . 1 (4 ounces)
Apples, dried . . . . 4 rings
Applesauce, unsweetened . . . . ½ cup
Apricots, canned . . . . ½ cup
Apricots, dried. 8 halves
Apricots, fresh . . . . 4 whole
                                        (5½ ounces)
Banana, small . . . . 1 (4 ounces)
Blackberries. . . . . ¾ cup
Blueberries . . . . ¾ cup
Cantaloupe, small . . . . ⅓ melon
                                        (11 ounces) or
                                        1 cup cubes

Cherries, sweet, canned. . . . . ½ cup
Cherries, sweet, fresh. . . . . 12 (3 ounces)
Dates. 3
Figs, dried 1½
Figs, fresh . . . . 1½ large or
                               2 medium
                                   (3½ ounces)

Fruit cocktail. . . . . ½ cup
Grapefruit, large . . . . ½ (11 ounces)
Grapefruit sections, canned . . . . ¾ cup
Grapes, small . . . . 17 (3 ounces)
Honeydew melon . . . . 1 slice (10 ounces)
                                 or 1 cup cubes
Kiwifruit . . . . 1 (3½ ounces)
Mandarin oranges, canned . . . . ¾ cup
Mango, small . . . . ½ fruit
                                 (5½ ounces)
                                 or ½ cup
Nectarine, small . . . . 1 (5 ounces)
Orange, small . . . . 1 (6½ ounces)
Papaya. . . . . ½ fruit (8 ounces)
                                 or 1 cup cubes
Peach, medium, fresh . . . . 1 (6 ounces)
Peaches, canned . . . . ½ cup
Pear, large, fresh . . . . ½ (4 ounces)
Pears, canned . . . . ½ cup
Pineapple, canned. . . . . ½ cup
Pineapple, fresh. ¾ cup
Plums, canned. . . . . ½ cup
Plums, small . . . . 2 (5 ounces)
Prunes, dried. 3
Raisins. . . . . 2 tablespoons
Raspberries . . . . 1 cup
Strawberries, whole berries . . . . 1¼ cups

Tangerines, small. . . . . 2 (8 ounces)
Watermelon. . . . . 1 slice
                                                (13½ ounces)
                                                    or 1¼ cups
                                                    cubes

Fruit Juice

Apple juice/cider . . . . ½ cup
Cranberry juice cocktail . . . . ⅓ cup
Cranberry juice cocktail,
      reduced-calorie. . . . . 1 cup
Fruit-juice blends, 100% juice . . . . ⅓ cup
Grape juice . . . . ⅓ cup
Grapefruit juice. ½ cup
Orange juice . . . . ½ cup
Pineapple juice . . . . ½ cup
Prune juice . . . . ⅓ cup

Milk List

Each serving of milk or milk product in this list contains about 12 grams of carbohydrate and 8 grams of protein. The amount of fat in the milk (0–8 grams per serving) determines whether it is identified as skim/very low fat milk, low-fat milk, or whole milk. In general, one milk is 1 cup.

Skim and Very Low Fat Milk (0–3 Grams Fat Per Serving)

Evaporated skim milk . . . . ½ cup
½% milk . . . . 1 cup
Nonfat dry milk. ⅓ cup (dry)
Nonfat or low-fat buttermilk. . . . . 1 cup

Nonfat or low-fat fruit-flavored yogurt
    sweetened with aspartame or
    with a nonnutritive sweetener. . . . . . . 1 cup
1% milk . . . . 1 cup
Plain nonfat yogurt . . . . ¾ cup
Skim milk . . . . 1 cup

Low-Fat
(5 Grams Fat Per Serving)

Plain low-fat yogurt . . . . ¾ cup
Sweet acidophilus milk . . . . 1 cup
2% milk . . . . 1 cup

Whole Milk
(8 Grams Fat Per Serving)

Evaporated whole milk . . . . ½ cup
Goat's milk . . . . 1 cup
Kefir . . . . 1 cup
Whole milk . . . . 1 cup

Other Carbohydrates

This group of foods allows for substitution of any food choice on
the list for a starch, or a fruit, or a milk in the meal plan. These
foods can be substituted even though they contain added sugars
or fat. Because many of these foods are concentrated sources of
carbohydrate and fat, the portion sizes are usually small.

Food	Serving Size	Exchanges Per Serving
Angel food cake, unfrosted . . .	¹⁄₁₂ cake	2 carbohydrates
Brownie, small, unfrosted . .	2-inch square	1 carbohydrate, 1 fat

Cake, frosted	2-inch square	2 carbohydrates, 1 fat
Cake, unfrosted	2-inch square	1 carbohydrate, 1 fat
Cookie, fat-free.	2 small	1 carbohydrate
Cookie or sandwich cookie with cream filling	2 small	1 carbohydrate, 1 fat
Cranberry sauce, jellied	¼ cup	2 carbohydrates
Cupcake, frosted.	1 small	2 carbohydrates, 1 fat
Doughnut, glazed	3¾ inches across (2 ounces)	2 carbohydrates, 2 fats
Doughnut, plain cake.	1 medium (1½ ounces)	1½ carbohydrates, 2 fats
Fruit juice bars, frozen, 100% juice	1 bar (3 ounces)	1 carbohydrate
Fruit snacks, chewy (pureed fruit concentrate) . . .	1 roll	1 carbohydrate (¾ ounce)
Fruit spreads, 100% fruit. . . .	1 tablespoon	1 carbohydrate
Gelatin, regular	½ cup	1 carbohydrate
Gingersnaps	3	1 carbohydrate
Granola bar	1 bar	1 carbohydrate, 1 fat
Granola bar, fat-free	1 bar	2 carbohydrates
Hummus	⅓ cup	1 carbohydrate, 1 fat
Ice cream	½ cup	1 carbohydrate, 2 fats
Ice cream, fat-free, no sugar added	½ cup	1 carbohydrate

Ice cream, light	½ cup	1 carbohydrate, 1 fat
Jam or jelly, regular	1 tablespoon	1 carbohydrate
Milk, chocolate, whole	1 cup	2 carbohydrates, 1 fat
Pie, fruit, 2 crusts	⅙ pie	3 carbohydrates, 2 fats
Pie, pumpkin or custard	⅛ pie	1 carbohydrate, 2 fats
Potato chips	12–18 (1 ounce)	1 carbohydrate, 2 fats
Pudding, regular (made with low-fat milk)	½ cup	2 carbohydrates
Pudding, sugar-free (made with low-fat milk)	½ cup	1 carbohydrate
Salad dressing, fat-free	¼ cup	1 carbohydrate
Sherbet, sorbet	½ cup	2 carbohydrates
Spaghetti or pasta sauce, canned	½ cup	1 carbohydrate, 1 fat
Sweet roll or Danish	1 (2½ ounces)	2½ carbohydrates, 2 fats
Syrup, light	2 tablespoons	1 carbohydrate
Syrup, regular	1 tablespoon	1 carbohydrate
Syrup, regular	¼ cup	4 carbohydrates
Tortilla chips	6–12 (1 ounce)	1 carbohydrate, 2 fats
Yogurt, frozen, fat-free, no sugar added	½ cup	1 carbohydrate
Yogurt, frozen, low-fat, fat-free	⅓ cup	1 carbohydrate, 0–1 fat
Yogurt, low-fat with fruit	1 cup	3 carbohydrates, 0–1 fat
Vanilla wafers	5	1 carbohydrate, 1 fat

Meat and Meat Substitutes List

Very Lean Meat and Substitutes

Poultry: Chicken or turkey (white meat,
no skin), Cornish hen (no skin) . . . . . 1 ounce

Fish: Fresh or frozen cod, flounder,
haddock, halibut, trout, tuna (fresh or
canned in water) . . . . 1 ounce

Shellfish: Clams, crab, lobster, scallops,
shrimp, imitation shellfish . . . . 1 ounce

Game: Duck or pheasant (no skin),
venison, buffalo, ostrich . . . . 1 ounce

Cheese: with 1 gram or less fat per ounce
Nonfat or low-fat cottage cheese. . . . . ¼ cup
Fat-free cheese . . . . 1 ounce

Other: Processed sandwich meats with 1 gram or less
fat per ounce, such as
deli-thin, shaved meats, chipped beef,
turkey ham. . . . . 1 ounce
Egg substitutes, plain . . . . ¼ cup
Egg whites 2
Hot dogs with 1 gram or less fat
per ounce. . . . . 1 ounce
Kidney (high in cholesterol) . . . . . . 1 ounce
Sausage with 1 gram or less fat
per ounce. . . . . 1 ounce

Lean Meat and Substitutes

Beef: USDA Select or Choice grades of lean beef trimmed of
fat, such as round, sirloin, and flank steak;
tenderloin; roast (rib, chuck, rump);
steak (T-bone, porterhouse, cubed),
ground round. . . . . 1 ounce

Pork: Lean pork, such as fresh ham; canned,
cured, or boiled ham; Canadian bacon;
tenderloin, center-loin chop . . . . 1 ounce
Lamb: Roast, chop, leg . . . . 1 ounce
Veal: Lean chop, roast. . . . . 1 ounce
Poultry: Chicken, turkey (dark meat, no
skin), chicken white meat (with skin),
domestic duck or goose (well drained
of fat, no skin) . . . . 1 ounce
Fish:
Herring (uncreamed or smoked) . . . . 1 ounce
Oysters. . . . . 6 medium
Salmon (fresh or canned), catfish. . . . 1 ounce
Sardines (canned) . . . . 2 medium
Tuna (canned in oil, drained) . . . . . . 1 ounce
Game: Goose (no skin), rabbit . . . . 1 ounce
Cheese:
Cheeses with 3 grams or less fat
per ounce. . . . . 1 ounce
4.5% fat cottage cheese. . . . . ¼ cup
Grated Parmesan . . . . 2 tablespoons
Other:
Hot dogs with 3 grams or less fat
per ounce. . . . . 1½ ounces
Liver, heart (high in cholesterol) . . . . 1 ounce
Processed sandwich meat with 3 grams
or less fat per ounce, such as turkey
pastrami or kielbasa . . . . 1 ounce

Medium-Fat Meat and Substitutes

Beef: Most beef products fall into this
category (ground beef, meatloaf,
corned beef, short ribs, Prime grades
of meat trimmed of fat, such as
prime rib). 1 ounce

Pork: Top loin, chop, Boston butt, cutlet . . 1 ounce
Lamb: Rib roast, ground . . . . 1 ounce
Veal: Cutlet (ground or cubed,
     unbreaded) . . . . 1 ounce
Poultry: Chicken dark meat (with skin),
     ground turkey, or ground chicken,
     fried chicken (with skin) . . . . 1 ounce
Fish: Any fried-fish product . . . . 1 ounce
Cheese: With 5 grams or less fat per ounce
     Feta . . . . 1 ounce
     Mozzarella . . . . 1 ounce
     Ricotta . . . . ¼ cup (2 ounces)
Other:
     Egg (high in cholesterol, limit to 3
       per week) 1
     Sausage with 5 grams or less fat per
       ounce . . . . 1 ounce
     Soy milk . . . . 1 cup
     Tempeh . . . . ¼ cup
     Tofu . . . . 4 ounces or ½ cup

HIGH-FAT MEAT AND SUBSTITUTES

Pork: Spareribs, ground pork, pork
     sausage . . . . 1 ounce
Cheese: All regular cheeses, such as
     American, cheddar, Monterey Jack,
     Swiss . . . . 1 ounce
Other: Processed sandwich meats with 8 grams or less fat per
     ounce, such as
       bologna, pimiento loaf, salami . . . . 1 ounce
       Bacon . . . . 3 slices
                             (20 slices/lb)
       Hot dog (turkey or chicken) 1 (10/lb)
       Sausage such as bratwurst, Italian,
         knockwurst, Polish, smoked . . . . 1 ounce

Fat List

Monounsaturated Fats

Avocado, medium . . . . ⅛ (1 ounce)
Oil (canola, olive, peanut) . . . . 1 teaspoon
Olives: Green, stuffed . . . . 10 large
      Ripe (black) . . . . 8 large
Nuts
      Almonds, cashews . . . . 6 nuts
      Mixed (50 percent peanuts) . . . . 6 nuts
      Peanuts . . . . 10 nuts
      Pecans . . . . 4 halves
Peanut butter, smooth or crunchy . . . . 2 teaspoons
Sesame seeds . . . . 1 tablespoon
Tahini paste . . . . 2 teaspoons

Polyunsaturated Fats

Margarine: stick, tub, or squeeze . . . . 1 teaspoon
      Lower-fat (30%–50% vegetable oil) . . . 1 tablespoon
Mayonnaise: regular . . . . 1 teaspoon
      Reduced fat . . . . 1 tablespoon
Miracle Whip Salad Dressing®: regular . . . 2 teaspoons
      Reduced fat . . . . 1 tablespoon
Nuts, walnuts, English . . . . 4 halves
Oil (corn, safflower, soybean) . . . . 1 teaspoon
Salad dressing: regular . . . . 1 tablespoon
      Reduced fat . . . . 2 tablespoons
Seeds: pumpkin, sunflower . . . . 1 tablespoon

Saturated Fats

Bacon, cooked . . . . 1 slice (20 slices/lb)
Bacon, grease . . . . 1 teaspoon

Butter: stick . . . . 1 teaspoon
    Reduced fat . . . . 1 tablespoon
    Whipped . . . . 2 teaspoons
Chitterlings, boiled . . . . 2 tablespoons
    (½ ounce)
Coconut, sweetened, shredded . . . . 2 tablespoons
Cream, half-and-half . . . . 2 tablespoons
Cream cheese: regular. . . . . 1 tablespoon
    (½ ounce)
    Reduced fat . . . . 2 tablespoons
    (1 ounce)
Shortening or lard . . . . 1 teaspoon
Sour cream: regular. . . . . 2 tablespoons
    Reduced fat . . . . 3 tablespoons

INDEX